The Vegetable Gardener's
Ultimate A–Z

Edward C. Smith

The Vegetable Gardener's
Ultimate A–Z

comprehensive sowing & growing guide to success with vegetables & herbs

Edward C. Smith

David and Charles

Interior photographs by Giles Prett, except for
those noted below.
   ©Sylvia Ferry Smith: pages 6 (bottom left), 8,
9 (middle), 21 (top), 45 (right and bottom), 64,
69, 70, 72, 75, 76 (bottom), 77, 82, 84, 85, 86 (top
right), 87, 88, 100, 101, 112, 123, 124 (top left
and right); ©David Cavagnaro: pages 61 and 107;
©Christine DuPuis: pages 61 and 91.
Illustration on page 47 by Brigita Fuhrmann

A DAVID & CHARLES BOOK

Copyright © Edward C. Smith 2000, 2004, 2007
Layout and design © David & Charles

First published in the UK by David & Charles as *The
Vegetable Gardener's Bible* in 2004
New edition 2007
David & Charles is an F+W Publications Inc.
company
4700 East Galbraith Road
Cincinnati, OH 45236

Originally published as *The Vegetable Gardener's Bible*
in the United States by Storey Publishing, LLC

Edward C. Smith has asserted his right to be
identified as author of this work in accordance
with the Copyright, Designs and Patents Act, 1988.

A catalogue record for this book is available from the
British Library.

ISBN-13: 978-0-7153-2742-5 wiro
ISBN-10: 0-7153-2742-9 wiro

Printed in China by Shenzen R R Donnelly Printing Co Ltd
for David & Charles
Brunel House   Newton Abbot   Devon

Commissioning Editor Jane Trollope
Assistant Editor Emily Rae
Designer Eleanor Stafford
Production Controller Beverley Richardson

Visit our website at www.davidandcharles.co.uk

David & Charles books are available from all
good bookshops; alternatively you can contact
our Orderline on 0870 9908222 or write to us at
FREEPOST EX2 110, D&C Direct, Newton Abbot,
TQ12 4ZZ (no stamp required UK only).

Contents

LAST THINGS FIRST:
Ripeness is All

Before we start, I want to consider the odd fact that ripeness means one thing to the vegetable plant and quite a different thing to the gardener. For plants, ripeness is most often a measure of the maturity of the seeds. The riper the fruit, the more viable the seeds will be. After all, a vegetable's idea of a successful life is to make seeds that will eventually sprout and carry on the family name. But to us gardeners, ripeness is when we find the fruit most desirable, whether the seeds are mature or not. Here are some examples of what I mean:

▸ **Tomatoes**. A ripe tomato has mature seeds, so it's technically ripe from the plant's point of view. It is also at its peak of juiciness and flavour, so it's ripe from my viewpoint, too.
▸ **Beans**. When the seeds of a French bean are ripe and mature, the bean has more in common with a leather belt than dinner. To me, a ripe French bean is slender with tiny seeds.

▸ **Squash**. Squash plants and I agree on ripeness for winter squash, but not for summer squash (courgettes), which are tastiest when very small and tender, with immature seeds.
▸ **Peppers**. Pepper plants agree with my notion of ripeness when my taste runs to red fruits, but not when I prefer them green.

WHEN RIPE IS RIPE

We harvest portions other than the fruits of some plants, such as onions, garlic and potatoes. These crops are ripe when the plant wilts or dies back – signs that are pretty easy to see. But the signs of ripeness are not so dramatic and obvious with some other plants, such as tomatoes and melons, whose fruit we harvest. The signs of ripeness in these crops are much more subtle. Instead of affecting the entire plant, signals of the perfect time to pick are often restricted to the area just around the ripening fruit. For example, when a tomato or

Plants that are tastiest when their seeds are ripe

△ **Hot tomato!** When tomatoes are most juicy and flavourful, their seeds are also mature. Not only does a ripe tomato colour up nicely, but it comes away easily from the vine when gently tugged.

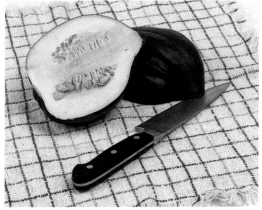

△ **Winning winter squash.** Unlike courgettes, which are best when their seeds are small and unformed, winter squash is most tasty when its seeds are mature.

melon ripens on the vine, the plant is healthy, green and vigorous, but the stem holding the ripe fruit begins to change, turning yellowish and loosening its grip on the fruit. A fully ripe tomato will slip loose from the plant if lifted gently. A ripe cantaloupe melon will come free from the plant with a gentle push of your thumb against the stem. One melon that gives a different readiness signal is the Charentais: you can tell that it's ripe when the small leaf next to the melon turns light brown.

Of course ripeness can usually be gauged by looking at the fruit. Tomatoes, and many other vegetables, change colour noticeably as they ripen. Some crops, such as tomatoes, are forgiving as well and will ripen even if they are picked before they reach their peak. Others, such as strawberries, must be picked when absolutely ripe as they will not ripen further after being harvested.

△ **Seedy and down at heel.** The oversized, seedy marrow on the left doesn't compare in texture or flavour with its tender sister, the courgette, on the right. As these vegetables mature, not only do the seeds become large and tough, but the area around them becomes stringy, soft and flavourless.

Plants that die back when they are mature

△ **Onion family signals.** You'll know it's time to harvest garlic and onions when their tops brown and flop over.

△ **One potato, two potatoes.** Get ready to dig your potatoes when you see the tops wilt and die back.

TWO KINDS OF RIPE

Sometimes ripe is simply a matter of personal taste. When is a pepper ripe? Or a green bean? Or a turnip? In each case, there's more than one right answer.

Peppers. Bell-type peppers are edible when they're green and immature, but they may be red, yellow, orange or brown when they mature, and they're edible at every stage between their green and fully coloured states. Mature peppers are sweet, while green peppers are tangy. Harvest them when they taste good to you. Picking peppers at the green stage means you'll end up with a bigger crop per plant, because if you keep picking the fruits before they ripen fully the plant goes on making new ones.

Green beans that are to be eaten fresh or preserved by freezing taste best early in their development, long before the seeds in the pods are fully grown. Beans that grow much beyond the diameter of a pencil quickly lose tenderness and taste. Then when they get really big ('ripe' from the bean plant's view of things), they are edible again. At that stage, however, it's not the pods you eat, but the tasty seeds.

Root crops. Turnips, as well as beetroot and carrots, have multiple 'ripenesses' depending on what you plan to do with them. Turnips and beetroot can be called ripe very early in life and cooked along with their leaves. They are all most tender, tasty and sweet at medium sizes, but they store better if they're bigger.

THE MORE YOU TAKE, THE MORE YOU GET

Call it the harvest paradox: the more courgettes, cucumbers, peas or green and yellow beans you pick, the more you get to pick. A pea plant's goal in life is not to produce small, tender sweet peas to feed us, but to produce big, tough, starchy, inedible peas that will be the seeds for next year's pea plants. As soon as

△ **Pick a peck.** You can harvest and enjoy bell peppers throughout their growing stages. A young green pepper will have more of a tang than a fully mature, sweet red pepper.

Jumping the Gun

You can harvest some onions (not garlic) and potatoes early in the season and enjoy special treats that only gardeners usually do:

▶ Plant some onion sets or plants very close together and then eat the thinnings as spring onions or little bulb onions.

▶ Reach into the soil beneath a potato plant and filch a few tubers when the peas are ready. New potatoes and tender young peas with butter make a delicious dish.

a pea plant succeeds in producing some seed-sized peas, its mission is accomplished, and it stops producing any more food-sized peas for you and me. The same is true of marrows, cucumbers and beans. An easy way to increase your harvest is to harvest regularly, when the fruits are young and tender.

SEIZE THE MOMENT

Carrots are tasty from the time they're as big as your little finger to when they're full-sized, so the carrot harvest spans most of the summer. The flavour and nutritional value of carrots changes over time. Baby carrots taste better, but big carrots are more nutritious. Some vegetables are another matter entirely. A French bean that was too small yesterday may be too big tomorrow, making its harvest time today, and today only. If I want the best French beans, I pick all the ripe ones every day. Ordinary beans, peas, and marrows offer a larger window of opportunity, but I still check every day and pick at least every second day.

Salad radishes taste good to me when they're the size of little marbles, but by the time they're the size of big marbles they're close to splitting open and possibly becoming infested with root maggots. I try to harvest them all before this happens and store them in the refrigerator.

◁ **It's a pea-pickin' thing.** If you diligently keep pea and bean vines picked, they will continue to produce.

◁ **Marbles, anyone?** Pull and refrigerate radishes when they're still small. They keep longer and their flavour is better.

▽ **Sunny side up.** Young carrots are one of those gourmet treats that keep gardeners going. These early carrots are at their most tender, tasty stage, though carrots are higher in nutrients and store better when they're dug a bit later.

Artichokes

This gourmet vegetable is grown in warm climates as either a perennial or biennial but in cold climates as an annual. If that seems confusing to you, think how it must be for the artichoke. Native to the Mediterranean, artichokes (globe not Jerusalem) are becoming increasingly popular in vegetable gardens in other parts of the world. Their ideal spot is warm and sheltered and they thrive particularly in coastal areas. If conditions are unfavourable they will need some special care – but they're worth it.

△ **This bud's for dinner!** Who discovered the tender treat at the heart of this prickly vegetable? Growing artichokes successfully is almost as satisfying as eating them.

THE SITE

Where winter temperatures never go below about –10°C (14°F), artichokes can be grown as perennials, the way nature intended. During their first year, the plants make leaves, but no buds (the edible portion of the plant). The second year, they produce buds in late summer and autumn. In areas with warm, dry climates, buds may form all year long but they will be of best quality in the spring. In such areas, artichoke plants can produce buds for three to five years. In areas with a colder climate, you may have to fool Mother Nature to get your artichokes in one growing season.

Sow & Grow

ARTICHOKES

(Cynara scolymus)
Sunflower family (Compositae)

SOWING
Seed depth: 6mm (¼in)

Germination soil temperature: 21–27°C (70–80°F)

Days to germination: 10–14

Sow indoors: Late winter to early spring – 10 weeks before last frost

Sow outdoors: Not recommended

GROWING
pH range: 6.5–8.0

Growing soil temperature: 16–24°C (60–75°F)

Spacing in beds: 60cm (2ft)

Watering: Heavy

Light: 8 hours or more per day

Nutrient requirements: N=high; P=high; K=high

Rotation considerations: Avoid following Jerusalem artichoke, sunflower

Good companions: Sunflower, tarragon

Bad companions: None

Seed longevity: 5 years

Seeds per gram: 350 (10,000 seeds per oz)

SOWING

Sow seeds indoors in seed compost in trays or pots and set them in a 21–27°C (70–80°F) spot; the seedlings should appear in about 12 days. Transplant into 10cm (4in) pots as soon as the first set of true leaves begins to expand, reducing temperatures to 16–21°C (60–70°F) during the day and 10–16°C (50–60°F) at night. In warm regions, the plants will be ready for the garden when they are about six weeks old. Set them in the soil and cover with a polytunnel for a week or two. If you live in a cool region and need to treat them as annuals, follow the strategy in the box below.

You *Can* Fool Mother Nature

In cool regions, it's time to start the trickery when your artichoke plants are about six weeks old. The objective is to convince the artichoke that it is two years old and ready to make buds, rather than a seedling ready to make only leaves. This is done by growing the plant at cool temperatures for a prescribed length of time. This cold treatment makes the seedling behave like a two-year-old plant ready to flower.

Temperatures during the cold treatment should remain below 10°C (50°F) but above 2°C (35°) for at least 250 continuous hours (about 10½ days). Since it is difficult to prevent times when temperatures rise above 10°C (50°F), give the plants the cold treatment for an even longer period: from four to six weeks. Put the plants in a cold frame about six weeks before the last frost. Keep the frame open during the day for cooling and closed at night for frost protection.

When all danger of frost is past and the soil temperature is above 16°C (60°F), set plants about 60cm (2ft) apart in the bed.

GROWING

Fertilizing. Artichokes are deep-rooted, heavy feeders, and grow best in soil enriched with lots of compost. Fertilize the bed once a month with compost 'tea' or another organic liquid feed.

Watering. Water evenly throughout the plants' growing season.

HARVESTING AND STORING

A mature artichoke bud, ready for the dinner table, is firm, tight, and a nice even green colour. If it begins to open, the tenderness quickly deteriorates. The first bud to mature is the top, or terminal, bud, followed over the next few days by the lateral, or secondary, buds. The terminal bud is often a bit larger than most of the lateral ones, but they all taste good.

Using a sharp knife, cut the buds at the base during cool, moist weather for the best flavour. The buds can be stored in a refrigerator for up to two weeks.

PREPARING FOR WINTER

In warm regions. After harvest in late autumn, cut the plants at or just below ground level and cover with an organic mulch.

In cold regions. Cut the plants to about 30cm (12in) from the ground and mound a light organic mulch, such as dry leaves or oat straw, over the stumps. Cover everything with large inverted plant pots. Mulch some more and, if practical, drape with a rainproof cover. Good mulching can bring plants through some very harsh winters.

BEST VARIETIES

Green Globe has been considered the best variety to grow for years, and remains so, but it now has competition.

Imperial Star produces up to three times more buds per plant than Green Globe.

Violetta di Chioggia is an attractive and tasty purple variety.

Asparagus

Like the king who wanted only a little bit of butter on his bread, asparagus is not fussy. Just give it a good place to grow, offer the nourishment and water it needs, and keep the weeds away. Given this level of attention, an asparagus bed will provide you and your family with food fit for a king for many years to come.

THE SITE

Asparagus is a perennial plant. Since typical asparagus beds can remain productive for 15–20 years, you'll want to choose the site carefully. Too often, asparagus beds are located for the gardener's convenience instead of for the plants' needs.

If you're starting a new bed you should site it in the northern portion of the garden, so that the tall ferns won't shade other plants. Keep it away from the edge of the garden, too, so grass and weeds are less likely to creep in and get established.

△ **Tender loving care** results in an abundant harvest of sweet spring treats. For the best flavour, you've got to grow your own, because asparagus quickly loses its flavour after it's been cut.

Sow & Grow

ASPARAGUS
(Asparagus officinalis)
Onion family (Liliaceae)

SOWING/PLANTING
Seed depth: 6–13mm (¼–½in)
Germination soil temperature: 25°C (77°F)
Days to germination: 10–12
Sow indoors: 8 weeks before last frost
Plant outdoors: In spring, 3 weeks before last frost

GROWING
pH range: 6.5–7.5

Growing soil temperature: 16–24°C (60–70°F)
Spacing in beds: 45cm (18in)
Watering: Heavy
Light: 8 hours or more per day for best yield; will tolerate 4–8 hours
Nutrient requirements: N=high; P=moderate; K=moderate
Rotation considerations: Avoid following onion family plants
Good companions: Basil, calendula, parsley, tomato
Bad companions: Onion, chive, garlic, leek
Seed longevity: 3 years
Seeds per gram: 50 (1,400 seeds per oz)

Traditionally, asparagus crowns were planted in trenches that were 20–30cm (8–12in) deep. That was when open-pollinated varieties such as Martha Washington and Mary Washington were the most popular. Times have changed – and for the better. Research has produced the Jersey Series of all-male asparagus. These varieties are planted just 12.5–15cm (5–6in) deep and can yield up to four times as many spears as the older types.

PLANTING

If conditions allow, it is best to prepare the soil of your asparagus bed in the autumn if you wish to use it for planting the following spring. At a pinch, however, you can prepare a new bed in the spring if the pH of the soil is already within the recommended range. Cultivate the soil to a depth of about 40cm (16in) and work 2.5cm (1in) of compost into the top 7.5cm (3in) of the bed.

In most regions, you should plant your asparagus crowns in early spring, at about the time when daffodils are in bloom. In very warm areas however, planting in autumn or winter is preferred.

Getting the Acidity Right

Be sure to test your soil before you start planting. Asparagus does best in a slightly acid to slightly alkaline soil (6.5–7.5), a higher pH than you generally want in the rest of the garden. Dig any improvers deeply into the soil.

Planting Asparagus Crowns

1 Dig a hole about 30cm (12in) deep for open-pollinated varieties such as Martha Washington, and 15cm (6in) deep for Jersey hybrids such as Jersey Knight and Jersey King. Add about 2.5cm (1in) of compost to the bottom of the hole. Place plants 45cm (18in) apart. Don't crowd them; asparagus likes plenty of room.

2 Place the one-year-old crowns in the bottom of the hole, and spread the roots out evenly. Cover the crowns with 5cm (2in) of soil. As the ferns grow during the summer, gradually fill the hole with soil, but ensure that you add no more than 5–7.5cm (2–3in) at a time, until the hole is filled.

GROWING

Fertilizing. As far as vegetables go, asparagus has a pretty big appetite, with good reason. Because they are perennials, the plants need to produce enough energy to feed us, produce new ferns, and survive the winter. It may be possible to overfeed asparagus, but it isn't easy. To ensure a steady source of nutrients for the plants and keep soil organisms busy loosening and aerating the soil, make regular applications of compost or rotted manure throughout the growing season.

Weed control. If asparagus has to share nutrients with weeds, its vigour is affected and its yield and longevity is ultimately reduced. Around midsummer, apply a straw or hay mulch to help with weed control as well as to moderate the soil temperature and help with moisture conservation. Create a buffer zone between the bed and the garden edge by using an opaque mulch, such as layers of newspaper or cardboard covered with straw, to discourage invading grasses.

For asparagus, any competitor is a weed. This includes the asparagus seedlings that sprout from those red berries produced by open-pollinated varieties. Hoe them out, being careful not to damage the roots of the parent plants. Or you can avoid the pretty red berries entirely by growing all-male varieties such as Jersey Giant.

'Weeds' also include any potential companion plants. Tomatoes, for instance, are often mentioned as companions for asparagus, but tomatoes take a lot of nutrients from the soil.

HARVESTING

You can harvest fresh asparagus from the garden the second spring after planting (the third if you're starting from seeds). The first harvest should be light, no more than two or three spears per plant over a period of about two weeks. Each following spring, harvest spears that are more than 1cm (½in) in diameter and 15–20cm (6–8in) tall. Let the thinner spears grow into ferns to help develop the crowns. Stop harvesting when most of the emerging spears are small and the tips become loose and open; this will happen at about the time you start harvesting peas. A typical harvest lasts from four to eight weeks.

△ **Weed no more.** A thick straw mulch around asparagus plants holds down weeds and helps keep soil moist and cool.

△ **Nip them in the bud.** Loose tips, like the one on the left, mean stringy asparagus. Choose stalks like the one on the right with its nice, tight bud. Check your asparagus every day during the harvest season, so you don't miss the perfect picks.

There are two schools of thought on how to harvest: you can cut the spear at or just below the soil with a knife; or – my preference – bend the spear until it breaks, which leaves a bit of it above the soil.

STORING

You've got to be kidding. You don't store asparagus, you eat asparagus... immediately after cooking, or sooner if you count the half-dozen spears munched right in the garden.

If you must store asparagus, either immerse the newly harvested spears in a tub of cold water or stand the bunch in a shallow container filled with 2.5–5cm (1–2in) of cold water for a few minutes. Drain and refrigerate in plastic storage bags. It stays fresh for about a week. Storage temperature is important for asparagus; for best results, it must be just above 0°C (32°F).

PREPARING FOR WINTER

The thick growth of asparagus ferns, or brush, that covers the bed in late summer and early autumn turns brown and brittle at the end of the growing season. In early to mid-autumn, you can cut it back to the ground and add it to the compost heap.

Test the soil and add improvers to restore soil fertility and maintain a pH of about 7.0. Next, spread compost or rotted manure at least 2.5cm (1in) thick over the bed. Finish with a mulch of straw about 15cm (6in) deep. This both protects the asparagus crowns from winter damage and allows soil organisms to continue improving the soil, both in autumn and spring.

BEST VARIETIES

Open-pollinated types: Martha Washington and Mary Washington are both old-fashioned cultivars that reliably produce large crops.

Rutgers hybrids: Jersey Giant, Jersey Knight, and Jersey King are all-male varieties that produce huge crops of thick, tender spears.

△ **Bend or cut?** I prefer the bend-and-break method of harvesting asparagus because only the tenderest, most flavourful portion of the spear remains in my hand. If you cut the stalk with a knife, on the other hand, you get any tough parts as well.

Eat Now, Pay Later

Unlike other garden vegetables, which reward us only after we work all summer long to tend and nurture them, asparagus gives us the reward first. From the plant's perspective, however, the important part is still to come: it must grow lush and hardy ferns to make lots of food to store in its roots for the following spring. But we've already had what we want from the plant, and all too often we neglect it during what, for it, is a critically important time. Be fair to your asparagus: keep it well weeded, fertilized and watered throughout the growing season.

Aubergines

For northern gardeners, aubergines (eggplants) are fussy plants. We like them once they are on the dinner plate, but in the garden they can drive you batty. Most of the gardeners in my neck of the woods have given up trying to grow them – though some just go on trying year after year through sheer cussedness. If you garden in a warm climate, on the other hand, you no doubt already know what makes this plant happy. An aubergine's most pressing need is for warmth, and the weather must remain warm throughout the plant's growth cycle if it is to thrive. If you live in a climate with hot summers, the plant will be more forgiving than in regions with short, cool growing seasons. If you garden in a cooler area, you'll have to resort to a few tricks to have any kind of success with your aubergines.

△ **Putting your eggs in one basket.** Aubergines come in a surprising variety of sizes, shapes and colours, from tiny-fruited kinds the size of a hen's egg, to large pear-shaped kinds, to thin, cucumber-like varieties. All aubergines have a similar flavour, though some are milder than others.

Sow & Grow

AUBERGINE
(*Solanum melongena*)
Tomato family (Solanaceae)

SOWING
Seed depth: 6mm (¼in)
Germination soil temperature: 29°C (85°F)
Days to germination: 7
Sow indoors: 4–6 weeks before last frost
Sow outdoors: Not recommended

GROWING
pH range: 5.5–7.0
Growing soil temperature: 27–32°C (80–90°F)
Spacing in beds: 45cm (18in)
Watering: Heavy
Light: Full sun
Nutrient requirements: N=moderate; P=high; K=high
Rotation considerations: Follow bean, pea
Good companions: Dwarf bean, pea, pepper, potato
Bad companions: Fennel
Seed longevity: 4 years
Seeds per gram: 250 (7,000 seeds per oz)

SOWING

Start aubergines indoors eight weeks before transplanting. You'll want to time transplanting for when you can count on the following conditions: soil temperature of at least 21°C (70°F); daytime air temperature consistently above 21°C (70°F); night air temperature not below 16°C (60°F).

Aubergines are very sensitive to transplant shock, so instead of sowing seed in trays, start the plants off in 10cm (4in) pots, two or three seeds to a pot. Germinate with bottom heat and try to maintain a soil temperature of at least 27°C (80°F) until the seedlings emerge, and 21°C (70°F) thereafter. Thin to one plant per pot by cutting the extras with scissors. Brush the plants gently with your hand twice a day to promote stocky growth and hefty stems. Grow under lights if you have them. As the plants grow indoors, prepare their outdoor planting bed by warming it with plastic mulch.

Harden the seedlings for a week before transplanting by decreasing the air temperature to 16°C (60°F) and cutting back on water. Outdoors, cut slits in the plastic mulch and transplant carefully to avoid root damage.

GROWING

Once the plants are in the garden, use polytunnels along with the mulch, both to provide steady heat and to protect the plants from insect damage. Apart from the aubergine's need for heat, the other challenge in producing a good crop is protection from pests. Insects love aubergines. If there is only one flea beetle in our garden, it won't be on a cabbage plant: it will be on the aubergines. And so will thrips, aphids and many others. The good news is that, unlike many other plants, aubergines can be grown beneath polytunnels from transplant to harvest.

About a month before the first frost, snip off any remaining blossoms to encourage the existing fruits to ripen.

HARVESTING AND STORING

Harvest fruits any time after they've reached half their mature size. Not only are early-harvested aubergines more tender and less prone to bitterness, you'll also get a bigger total yield because keeping the plants picked stimulates further production. Cut the fruits from the plants with shears, leaving some stem attached. Eat them quickly because aubergines don't store well.

BEST VARIETIES

Diva. A traditional purple aubergine, Diva has thin skin and a mild flavour.

Asian Bride. Long, skinny, and pale white, like other Asian types, this variety has a subtle flavour and an unusually creamy texture.

Kermit. Small green and white fruits the size of a hen's egg are typical of Kermit's aubergine.

Machiaw. This aubergine looks like a blushing cucumber, with long, thin fruit brushed with rosy purple skin. It tastes good and yields very well.

Neon. Bright neon purple skin covers the tender, tasty flesh of Neon. Its yields are good and strikingly attractive to boot.

Rosa Bianca. Another attractive variety, Rosa Bianca has skin in shades of rose, lavender, and white that change throughout the season. Its flesh is sweet and mild.

Little Fingers. With lots of stout little purple fruits resembling fingers, this aubergine tastes wonderful. Harvest when fruit is small for best flavour.

There's a Lot at Stake

Although many varieties of aubergine grow into bushy plants about 60–90cm (2–3ft) tall and need no staking, some, including many of the thin-fruited Asian types, do best if grown on a frame or stake and pruned like indeterminate tomatoes.

Beetroot

Grown for their leaves as well as their roots, beetroot come in many colours and shapes. While it is technically true that those jars at the back of your cupboard contain beetroot, they aren't the best way to get to know this delicious vegetable. Beetroot baked in the oven like potatoes, or fresh baby beetroot and carrots sautéed in butter, are a better introduction to this flavourful, often overlooked vegetable.

THE SITE

Beetroot prefer a light soil with a pH of between 6.5 and 7.5. Research has shown that the roots of beetroot plants can grow down as much as 90cm (3ft) into the soil, a fact that emphasizes the benefits of gardening in deeply dug, wide, raised beds.

△ **Can't beat this.** Keep your beetroot cool by growing them under a mulch, and try to harvest them when they're no more than 6.5cm (2½in) in diameter. To avoid 'bleeding', remove the leaves by twisting rather than cutting.

Sow & Grow

BEETROOT

(Beta vulgaris) Crassa Group
Beet family (Chenopodiaceae)

SOWING

Seed depth: 13mm (½in)

Germination soil temperature: 24–29°C (75–85°F)

Days to germination: 5

Sow indoors: 5 weeks before last frost

Sow outdoors: 3–4 weeks before last frost

GROWING

pH range: 6.5–7.5

Growing soil temperature: 18–24°C (65–75°F)

Spacing in beds: *For greens,* 5cm (2in); *for summer use,* 7.5cm (3in); *for storage,* 10cm (4in)

Watering: Moderate and even

Light: Full sun for best yield; tolerates light shade

Nutrient requirements: N=low; P=moderate; K=moderate

Rotation considerations: Avoid following spinach or Swiss chard

Good companions: Butter bean, cabbage family, dwarf bean, lettuce, onion, radish, sweetcorn

Bad companions: Mustard, climbing bean

Seed longevity: 4 years

Seeds per gram: 70 (2,000 seeds per oz)

B

SOWING

Each beetroot 'seed' is actually a dried fruit containing a cluster of two to six seeds. Sow these seeds 5–10cm (2–4in) apart, a month or so before the last frost. Repeat sowings every two weeks until the last frost. If you sow beetroot in midsummer for winter storage, the soil is likely to be warmer than the seeds like. To improve germination, sow seeds at dusk or on a cool, cloudy day. Water well and add a thin dressing of compost to help moderate the soil temperatures.

After seedlings emerge, thin each cluster with floral shears or scissors. Save the most robust plant in each cluster and cut the rest at soil level. To avoid disturbing the remaining plants, don't pull out the unwanted seedlings.

GROWING

Plants that reach harvestable size during hot weather may have poor root colour and flavour. Beetroot grow best in cool conditions and profit from cooling mulches and companion-cropping with plants that shade the soil.

Watering. Even moisture, which allows steady, uninterrupted growth, is important if beetroot are to make tender eating. Be careful not to let the soil dry out.

Fertilizing. Too much nitrogen can result in luxuriant tops but poor root development. For best root growth, fertilize every three to four weeks with a low-nitrogen, organic fertilizer, high in phosphorus and potassium.

HARVESTING

Beetroot taste best when harvested at about 4–6.5cm (1½–2½in) in diameter. As the roots grow larger, they lose flavour and develop an unappetizing texture. To harvest, pull or dig the roots and remove the tops. Some people cut the leaves from the roots, but this can cause bleeding, which reduces the moisture content in the root. To minimize this, grasp the root

◁ **Sweet beetroot go deep.** Pulled from a deeply dug, sandy soil, this young specimen boasts a tap root of 30cm (12in). Its fine root hairs probed even further into the soil.

in one hand and the leaves in the other, and twist off the tops. Place in plastic vegetable bags and refrigerate, or store in damp sand in a cool place.

BEST VARIETIES

Miniature beetroot. Kleine Bol (Little Ball), Gladiator, Spinel, Pablo.
Speciality beetroot. Chioggia, Forono, Cyndor, Golden Beet.
Main-crop beetroot. Red Ace, Scarlet Supreme, Detroit Dark Red.

An Exception to Every Rule

In general, beetroot grow best in cool weather, but an extended cold snap – two or more weeks below 10°C (50°F) – occurring after beetroot plants have formed a rosette of leaves can force them to bolt; this ruins the quality of the roots. If a long cool period is expected you should place a floating plastic mulch over plants to keep daytime temperatures above 10°C (50°F).

Broccoli

You either love it or you don't. But lately, even people who don't love broccoli have found a good reason to learn to like it. Recent research has shown that broccoli contains large amounts of sulphoraphane, a compound that can prevent some types of cancer. And the good aspects of broccoli don't stop there. It also contains antioxidants, which help protect the body from some other diseases.

△ **Hale and hearty.** Broccoli is delicious and versatile, with health benefits as well.

The Site

Broccoli is a heavy user of nitrogen, so when planting choose a spot where fallen leaves were added the previous autumn. Don't start broccoli too early. Large or rootbound transplants may produce a tiny broccoli head, or 'button'. Discard these plants; they will not produce well. Long exposure to cold weather can also produce buttoning.

Sowing

Sow broccoli seeds about four to six weeks before the last spring frost. The seeds will germinate in about six days at 24°C (75°F). Once plants show true leaves, fertilize them with an organic liquid feed at half strength. For a second, or autumn, crop you can direct-sow in late spring in cool regions, and in summer in warm areas.

Sow & Grow

Broccoli

(Brassica oleracea) Italica Group, (B. rapa) Ruvo Group
Cabbage family (Cruciferae)

Sowing

Seed depth: 6mm (¼in)
Germination soil temperature: 27°C (80°F)
Days to germination: 4–7
Sow indoors: 6–8 weeks before last frost
Sow outdoors: Early summer for autumn crop

Growing

pH range: 6.5–7.5
Growing soil temperature: 16–18°C (60–65°F)

Spacing in beds: *Staggered pattern,* 40cm (16in); 3 rows to a wide bed (90cm; 36in)
Watering: Moderate and even
Light: Full sun for best yield; tolerates partial shade
Nutrient requirements: N=moderate to high; P=high; K=high
Rotation considerations: Avoid following with cabbage family plants
Good companions: Beetroot, carrot, celery, chard, cucumber, dill, dwarf bean, lettuce, mint, nasturtium, onion family, oregano, potato, rosemary, sage, spinach, tomato
Bad companions: Climbing and French beans, strawberry
Seed longevity: 3 years
Seeds per gram: 280 (8,000 seeds per oz)

GROWING

Broccoli transplants well, but be careful not to disturb the roots. Transplant when seedlings are about 7.5cm (3in) tall, and set plants 2.5cm (1in) deeper than they grew in the pots. Plant in a staggered pattern 40cm (16in) apart, with 30cm (12in) between rows. Three rows can fit in a bed 90cm (3ft) wide. The plants grow best when the soil pH is between 6.5 and 7.5.

Fertilizing. Every three to four weeks, rake in an organic fertilizer such as fish, blood and bonemeal. Broccoli, like all cabbage family relatives, needs significant amounts of boron, which tends to be deficient in very acid and alkaline soils and in soils with a low percentage of organic matter.

Broccoli-Raab

Broccoli-raab and broccoli are related, but you wouldn't confuse the two if you saw them side by side. While broccoli looks like, well, broccoli, broccoli-raab has thin, leafy shoots topped by small, loose clusters of buds. To grow broccoli-raab, sow indoors as for broccoli, or sow directly in the garden a week or two after peas are sown. Grow as broccoli until the shoots begin to sprout from the crown of the plant. When the shoots are about 30cm (12in) tall, harvest the buds and the few leaves just below them. The flavour of broccoli-raab is sharper than broccoli and is excellent when mixed with other vegetables. It can be tamed a bit by one change of water during boiling.

HARVESTING

Harvest when the head is dark green and fully formed; the buds should also be tight. Any hint of yellow colour in the buds is a sign that the head is overripe. Harvest by cutting the head free of the stalk with a knife. More, smaller heads will soon form as side shoots. Harvest these every few days to keep more forming. Some varieties, such as Early Packman, Saga, Mariner Hybrid, and Premium Crop, produce abundant side shoots.

◁ **Cut-and-come-again broccoli.** After the main head has been harvested (A), broccoli continues to produce side shoots (B) for several more weeks.

BEST VARIETIES

Broccoli varieties can be divided into a few handy groups: those that do best planted early in the season; those that will produce during summer; and those planted in summer for harvest in autumn or early winter. Choose from each group for a succession of crops.

Spring or early varieties. Early Dividend, Early Emerald and Early Packman.

Summer varieties. Genji, Mariner, Saga and Small Miracle.

Autumn or winter varieties. Arcadia, Marathon, Pirate and Saga.

Brussels Sprouts

If you grow Brussels sprouts, you'll be eating from the garden after most of the harvest is only a memory. They are one of the hardiest vegetables in the garden. Not only do they survive autumn frosts and light snowfalls, but the cold actually makes them taste better. This is one of the few vegetables that give cool-region gardeners an edge over their warm-region counterparts.

THE SITE

Brussels sprouts are tall plants reaching from 60–90cm (2–3ft), with thick stems and heavy bud production. Their root system, however, is close to the soil surface and, though dense, not very far reaching. These qualities mean Brussels sprouts require a rich, fertile soil and even moisture to grow at their best.

△ **Topping off.** About a month before you expect a hard freeze, top the plant by pinching out the growing tip. This directs all the plant's energy into maturing the remaining sprouts.

Sow & Grow

BRUSSELS SPROUTS

(Brassica oleracea)
Gemmifera Group
Cabbage family (Cruciferae)

SOWING

Seed depth: 6mm (¼in)

Germination soil temperature: 24–27°C (75–80°F)

Days to germination: 5–8

Sow indoors: 4–6 weeks before last frost

Sow outdoors: Early summer for autumn crop (warm regions)

GROWING

pH range: 6.0–6.8

Growing soil temperature: 16–18°C (60–65°F)

Spacing in beds: *Depending on type,* 40–45cm (16–18in); *staggered pattern,* 3 rows to a wide bed (90cm; 36in)

Watering: Moderate and even

Light: Full sun for best yield; tolerates light shade

Nutrient requirements: N=moderate; P=high; K=high

Rotation considerations: Avoid following cabbage family plants

Good companions: Beetroot, carrot, celery, cucumber, dwarf bean, lettuce, nasturtium, onion family, pea, potato, radish, spinach, tomato

Bad companions: Kohlrabi, climbing bean, strawberry

Seed longevity: 4 years

Seeds per gram: 300 (8,500 seeds per oz)

Prepare the bed in autumn by working in plenty of compost or well-rotted manure and autumn leaves. In spring, test the soil for nutrients and to be sure the pH is between 6.0 and 6.8. Brussels sprouts, like all cabbage family members, need significant amounts of boron. This micronutrient tends to be deficient in very acid soils, as well as in slightly alkaline soils and those with a low percentage of organic matter. If you are preparing the bed in spring, fork the soil well, add a layer of compost, and lightly turn the soil again.

SOWING

Even the shortest-season Brussels sprouts take a long time to grow (about 100 days), so start the plants indoors or in a cold frame about a month before the last frost date. Seeds will germinate in about a week at 24–27°C (75–80°F). Transplant when seedlings are from four to six weeks old. If your growing season is about four months long, Brussels sprouts can be direct-sown.

In areas that are entirely frost-free, direct-sow from mid-autumn to midwinter for harvest in spring. Sprouts grown in warm regions are often more open and have poorer flavour than those grown in cool areas.

GROWING

Brussels sprouts grow best in cool, evenly moist soil. Apply an organic mulch, such as straw, to moderate soil temperature during the warm months. Maintain a layer of compost on the bed under the mulch to supply nutrients and encourage the activity of worms. In areas exposed to persistent winds, plants may need staking. Insert stakes when transplants are planted to avoid damaging the roots of established plants.

Fertilizing. Fertilize every three to four weeks from transplanting to late summer with an organic fertilizer such as fish, blood and bonemeal. If your soil is rich, supplementary feeding may not be needed.

△ **Losing your marbles?** Get an early start on your Brussels sprouts harvest by picking the first, marble-sized buttons that form at the bottom of the plant. You'll be able to continue to harvest this vegetable long after the rest of the garden has been put away.

HARVESTING

Although the buttons improve in flavour after a frost or two, harvest whenever some are firm, between 'aggies' and 'shooter' marbles in size (13–25mm; ½–1in). Break off the leaf stem below the button and either snap or cut off the sprout.

If there are still sprouts left when night temperatures are near –4°C (25°F), cut the whole plant, strip the leaves, and hang it in a cool, damp place; the sprouts will be good for another three weeks.

BEST VARIETIES

Dwarf types, such as Jade Cross E and Oliver, produce harvests in less than 100 days. These varieties are excellent for cool regions where the growing season is short, as well as for very warm areas where the duration of cool weather is only a few months.

Tall varieties, such as Trafalgar and Valiant, usually take from 100 to 130 days to mature and are popular in more temperate parts of the world.

Cabbage

In some places, tradition holds that babies come from the cabbage patch. I know no one who has actually found this to be true, but it is easy to understand how the belief started. Cabbage isn't hard to grow, but it does need the right sort of attention to turn out well. Do this and, just as kids add joy to life, the cabbage patch will be one of the nicest, most rewarding parts of your garden.

THE SITE

Cabbage prefers a rich, fertile soil with a pH of 6.0 to 7.5, with the optimum about 6.5. It does best in full sun, especially in cool regions and other areas with short growing seasons. In warmer climates, cabbage tolerates light midday shade.

△ **C is for Cabbage.** Cabbage is easy to grow and delicious to eat either fresh or cooked. An excellent source of vitamin C, it's useful in dishes from many ethnic traditions. Shown here are a solid head (top) and a Savoy (bottom).

Sow & Grow

CABBAGE

(Brassica oleracea)
Capitata Group
Cabbage family (Cruciferae)

SOWING

Seed depth: 6mm (¼in)

Germination soil temperature: 24–29°C (75–85°F)

Days to germination: 5

Sow indoors: 4–6 weeks before last frost

Sow outdoors: 10–12 weeks before first frost for autumn crop

GROWING

pH range: 6.0–7.5 (7.2–7.5 to inhibit club root)

Growing soil temperature: 60–65°F (16–18°C)

Spacing in beds: *Early varieties,* 30cm (12in); *late varieties,* 45cm (18in)

Watering: Heavy from planting to head formation, then moderate

Light: Full sun for best yield; tolerates light shade

Nutrient requirements: N=high; P=high; K=high

Rotation considerations: Avoid following cabbage family plants

Good companions: Beetroot, carrot, celery, cucumber, dill, dwarf bean, lettuce, mint, nasturtium, onion family, potato, rosemary, sage, spinach, thyme

Bad companions: Climbing bean, strawberry, tomato

Seed longevity: 4 years

Seeds per gram: 250 (7,500 seeds per oz)

SOWING

Sow cabbage seeds for early crops in trays in early to mid-spring; sow late varieties in mid-spring. Once seedlings emerge, lower temperatures to about 16°C (60°). When the plants have a few true leaves, transplant directly from the seed tray to a 7.5cm (3in) pot. Transplant early-maturing varieties in early to mid-spring, spacing plants 30cm (12in) apart; transplant autumn varieties in early summer, spaced 45cm (18in) apart. Be careful not to disturb the rootball.

You can also direct-sow both early- and late-season cabbage, eliminating the possiblity of damaging the roots during transplanting. If you use this option, make sure that weeds don't crowd the seedlings, and use floating plastic mulches to discourage flea beetles.

GROWING

Fertilizing. All cabbages are heavy feeders and need ample, even supplies of most nutrients, including nitrogen, potassium, phosphorus and boron. Follow a nitrogen-fixing green-manure crop such as alfalfa. Best added to the soil in autumn or late winter, wood ashes are a good source of potassium and also help raise soil pH.

Mulching. Cabbage has a shallow, dense root system, with many feeder roots very close to the surface. The roots are easily damaged by everything from cultivation to fluctuations in soil moisture to high soil temperatures. A simple way to ensure a stress-free cabbage patch is to mulch. Mulches, including straw or salt hay and 'living mulch' (the shade provided by other crops, such as lettuce), reduce weeding as well as moderating soil temperature and moisture fluctuations.

Weeding. Early competition from weeds slows growth, particularly of direct-seeded plants, but cabbage roots are easily damaged by

---

No More Splits

Cabbages have a tendency to split and bolt. In general, any stress that disrupts growth after head formation can cause a head to split. These stresses include fluctuations in soil moisture and heads that have grown too large. There are several ways to slow growth and thus prevent splitting:

▶ Wait until just after the heads firm up, and then twist the plants to break some roots (A).

▶ Plunge the blade of a spade into the soil on one side of the plant (B).

▶ Reduce plant spacing. For early varieties of cabbage, space the plants 20–30cm (8–12in) apart; for late varieties, space plants 30–40cm (12–16in) apart. Heads will be smaller, but they will also have better flavour and be less likely to split.

▶ Plant a variety that is more resistant to splitting. Some good choices include Primax, Columbia, Dynamo, and Super Red 80.

cultivation, so use your hoe carefully or weed by hand. In fact, if a weed is big enough or close enough to the cabbage plant to cause damage when pulled, clip the weed with scissors. Avoid hoeing or working in the cabbage patch early in the morning, when leaves are full of moisture and brittle. Once heads begin to form, put the hoe away and do any weeding by hand.

HARVESTING AND STORING

Early cabbage. Early varieties do not store well and should be harvested for use any time after the head reaches the size of a grapefruit. The heads can grow larger, but they are most tender and tasty at this early stage, and the plant will often produce another head or heads, with the total harvest adding up to more than a single mature head would yield.

Late cabbage. Rather than cutting late crops grown for storage, pull them from the ground, roots and all. Remove the large leaves and all but a few wrapper leaves. Take care not to bruise the heads, as this will shorten their storage life. Late-season cabbage can tolerate some frosty nights before harvest. You have several different options for storing late cabbage:

▶ Cut off the roots and any loose or damaged leaves and place on shelves in a cool, damp, frost-free storage area.
▶ Prepare as above and wrap in newspaper; store as above.
▶ Hang by the roots in the store.
▶ Leave the roots on and lean the plants against the store wall, covering the roots with damp sand. If you use this method, you'll receive a little bonus when you get around to using the cabbage. After you have cut the head from the root, plant the root in a pot filled with damp sand and stand it on a sunny windowsill. Quite soon you'll be harvesting small cabbage leaves that you can use in salads, right in the middle of winter.

In general, green cabbage doesn't store as well as red varieties. Scanbo is an exception to this rule. Until we discovered Scanbo, our green cabbages never kept as well as the reds. Now it's a toss-up. I can't report on the storage quality of Savoy cabbages: we love the taste so much in late-autumn salads that the Savoys are always gone before we can compare storage times.

BEST VARIETIES

Early-season green: Dynamo has disease and split resistance and is a deserved prizewinner. Tendersweet has disease and split resistance, with a sweet flavour to boot.

Late-season green: Storage No. 4 and Scanbo are disease-resistant and store well.

Red: Rona is insect- and disease-tolerant, stores well, and has a mild flavour. Super Red 80 is split-resistant, with an excellent flavour.

Savoy: Prize-winning Savoy King has excellent flavour and is split-resistant. Wirosa is a high-quality, long-season cabbage that stores well.

Two Heads are Better than One

To extend your early-cabbage harvest you can try making one plant produce more than one head. When a cabbage head is ready to harvest, carefully cut it from the stalk, just below the head, leaving a stump. Cut a cross pattern into the stalk, making the slice about 6mm (¼in) deep. In a little while, up to four small heads will begin to appear. Harvest these when the heads are about the size of apples.

Carrots

If you are just now making the transition to deeply worked, raised garden beds, use the first of your new beds for carrots. The difference in size, shape, flavour and yield between row-crop and raised-bed carrots are – putting it mildly – dramatic. Like the carrot on the stick that keeps the horse going forward, the beautiful carrots you pull from your first raised bed will encourage you to grow all your vegetables this way.

THE SITE

Prepare and enrich the bed in autumn by forking in a layer of fallen leaves. If you're preparing the bed in spring, mix in a generous amount of compost a few weeks before seeding. Rake and smooth the bed carefully.

SOWING

Carrots can germinate in a week with a soil temperature at about 24°C (75°F). The

△ **A 24-carat vegetable.** When carrots are stored, they often lose their moisture and sweetness. What better reason to grow your own? Once you've experienced the pleasure of pulling those slender beauties from the earth, you're sure to be hooked.

Sow & Grow

CARROTS

(Daucus carota var. sativus)
Carrot family (Umbelliferae)

SOWING

Seed depth: 6–13mm (¼–½in)

Germination soil temperature: 24°C (75°F)

Days to germination: 6

Sow indoors: Not recommended

Sow outdoors: Early spring to midsummer

GROWING

pH range: 5.5–6.5, but best above 6.0

Growing soil temperature: 16–21°C (60–70°F)

Spacing in beds: *In rows,* 5cm (2in); *rows apart,* 15–20cm (6–8in); 3 rows to a 75cm (30in) bed, 4 rows to a 90cm (36in) bed

Watering: Moderate

Light: Full sun for best yield; tolerates light shade

Nutrient requirements: N=high; P=low; K=low

Rotation considerations: Avoid rotating with celery, dill, fennel, parsley, parsnip

Good companions: Bean, Brussels sprout, cabbage, chive, leaf lettuce, leek, onion, pea, pepper, red radish, rosemary, sage, tomato

Bad companions: Celery, dill, parsnip

Seed longevity: 3 years

Seeds per gram: 750 (22,000 seeds per oz)

colder the soil temperature, the longer the germination period. If it gets much below 7°C (45°F), germination may not happen at all. Plan to sow carrots at the same time you sow beans or tomatoes.

Carrot seeds are tiny and devilishly hard to space evenly. Over the years gardeners have come up with a number of solutions to this problem. I've tried many of them but wasn't really happy with results. The easiest way to sow carrots is to broadcast them over the bed. This method takes only seconds to accomplish but the eventual thinning of seedlings can take hours. I've tried mixing the seeds with dry coffee grounds or vermiculite before sowing. That was an improvement, but I still found the spacing somewhat irregular. Pelleted seeds are easy to handle and space but add another layer of material that the germinating seeds must push through before reaching daylight. Seed tapes look like a convenient idea but are too expensive for my liking. After experimenting with many ways to sow carrot seed, I've resorted to patiently sowing them one or two at a time as shown in the photo below.

One for Now, One for Later
Plant a quick-maturing variety for summer eating as soon as you like, but postpone planting the winter storage crop until the soil warms up, about the time you plant tomatoes.

GROWING

No matter how carefully I space the seeds, carrots always seem to need some thinning. They can grow very close together and still produce excellent crops, but if they grow too close together they'll be stunted, excessively slender, or deformed.

Carrots prefer their roots to be cool and their tops to be warm. When the soil temperature rises above 21°C (70°F) they will be small and bland tasting. To give carrots the growing conditions they like, add a layer of organic mulch, such as grass clippings, around the plants to moderate the soil temperature when the warmer days of late spring and summer arrive. Repeat as needed throughout the

△ **Practise makes perfect.** With a little practise, you can sow the seeds 13mm (½in) apart by rolling them, a half dozen or so at a time, between your thumb and first finger, so that just one (or sometimes two) will emerge at a time.

△ **Easy does it.** Thinning carrots, rather like sowing them, is best accomplished on days when patience can rule your actions. Thin with floral shears, leaving no less than 5cm (2in) between the individual plants.

growing season. In addition to using mulch, grow a leafy companion crop, such as Swiss chard, which will help shade and cool the soil.

HARVESTING AND STORING

In loose soil, carrots can be gathered by pulling them from the ground by their tops. If the tops break, loosen the soil carefully with a fork.Cut the leaves about 2.5cm (1in) from the roots. Cull any damaged or misshapen roots; they won't store well. Layer storage carrots in damp sand in a cool, frost-free place.

BEST VARIETIES

Nantes: A old favourite of gardeners, these sweet, crisp, full-flavoured carrots are easily recognized by their cylindrical shape and blunt tip. Some excellent varieties include Bolero, Napoli, Sweetness II, Nelson, Mokum and Scarlet Nantes.

Imperator: This is the long, tapering supermarket carrot. Easy to harvest and transport (which means little to gardeners), Imperators have poorer flavour and crispness than many other types. Some of the best varieties in this group, including Nevis and Artist, are actually Nantes hybrids.

Baby or Mini: These tasty, small carrots, with a range of shapes, are best used when they are fresh. This type is a bit of a catch-all category, since, if it's little, it can go here. Some popular varieties include Thumbelina, Minicore, Amsdor, and Parmex.

Chantenay: All-purpose carrots with a broad shoulder, stocky build, and blunt tip, Chantenays keep their shape better in stony or heavy soils than other carrots. Some varieties include Chantenay Red-Cored, Chantenay Royal and Chantenay Imperial.

Danvers: These good all-round carrots are similar in shape to Chantenay, but longer. Their flavour is good, but lacks the sweetness of Nantes. Some good varieties include Danvers Red-Cored and Danvers Half-Long.

△ **Long life.** Carrots store best if you cut off the leaves, leaving about 2.5cm (1in) of stem.

△ **Hidden treasure.** Carrots grown in deeply dug beds will be larger, more shapely, and tastier than you can imagine.

Give Your Carrots Some Friends

Because of their extremely small size, carrot seeds produce tiny seedlings that do not have the strength to push through crusted soil. You can help the little seedlings out by:

▶ Interplanting them with radishes. The radishes will emerge first and break up crusted surface soil.

▶ Keeping the soil moist throughout the germination period. This keeps the soil from crusting.

Climbing Beans

Flavour is always a debatable point, but most people who grow both dwarf and climbing (pole) beans think climbing beans are the sweeter, more tender and better tasting of the two. There is no debate regarding yield. Climbing beans produce more pods per plant than dwarf beans, and they're much easier to pick.

SOWING AND GROWING

Most of the growing information that applies to dwarf beans (see page 40) also works for climbing beans, with a few exceptions. Because these beans are climbing plants (called indeterminate), they need to be supported in order to help them produce the best crops. You can construct a frame from canes or netting, or

△ **Beans by the pyramid-full.** Climbing beans continue to grow, flower and produce pods over six to eight weeks, much longer than dwarf beans.

Sow & Grow

CLIMBING BEANS
(Phaseolus vulgaris)
Pea family (Leguminosae)

SOWING
Seed depth: 2.5cm (1in)
Germination soil temperature: 24–29°C (75–85°F)
Days to germination: 7–10
Sow indoors: Not recommended
Sow outdoors: When soil temperature reaches 16°C (60°F)

GROWING
pH range: 6.5–7.5
Growing soil temperature: 16–18°C (60–65°F)

Spacing in beds: *In groups* (for canes), 40cm (16in) apart, 4 plants per group; *in rows* (for frames), 7.5cm (3in) apart
Watering: Low at sowing, medium at flowering, heavy through harvest
Light: Full sun for best yield; tolerates light shade
Nutrient requirements: N=Low; P=moderate; K=moderate
Rotation considerations: Precede sweetcorn; avoid following pea and dwarf bean
Good companions: Aubergine, carrot, cauliflower, chard, cucumber, marigold, pea, potato, rosemary, strawberry, sweetcorn
Bad companions: Basil, beetroot, cabbage, fennel, kohlrabi, onion family, radish, sunflower
Seed longevity: 3 years
Seeds per gram: 3 (100 seeds per oz)

The vines will climb twine, canes or netting. For twine or canes, plant seeds in groups of four to six with 40cm (16in) between the groups. For netting, plant seeds 7.5cm (3in) apart, with a row on each side of the netting; stagger the rows. Anchor the netting or twine firmly in the ground with stakes or loops of heavy wire.

HARVESTING AND STORING

Climbing beans tend to stay tender on the vine longer than dwarf beans, but regular picking is still required to extend the harvest to its limit. When you have all the beans you need, let the remaining pods mature and use them like flageolet beans.

Climbing beans freeze very well, keeping a firmer texture than dwarf beans.

△ **From small beginnings.** Sow a handful of four to six seeds spaced around each cane.

BEST VARIETIES

Blue Lake. If you could call a bean variety tried-and-true, Blue Lake would definitely be the one. Tender and stringless, these beans stay tasty even when big.

Emerite. For flavour, it is hard to beat Emerite, a French filet bean with a deliciously sweet, nutty taste.

Gold Marie. This is a wax (yellow) bean with an excellent flavour.

Fortex. An extremely vigorous variety, Fortex also bears beans with a fine flavour.

Jack never had it this good. ▷ This rustic obelisk makes a sturdy and attractive support for beanstalks as well as for other climbing plants.

Cauliflower

Cauliflower has long had a reputation for being a prima donna in the vegetable world. It is the easiest of the cabbage family vegetables to stress, and when it does becomes stressed, it acts like a two year old and bolts. Cauliflower can be set back by cool temperatures in spring, hot weather in summer, or dry conditions at any time. And to top everything off, of all the members of the cabbage family, it's the most sensitive to frost. Altogether, cauliflower could be called the black sheep of the cabbage family, but we still love it and regard it as a challenge to grow it well.

△ **Flower power.** Harvested at its prime, cauliflower has a sweet, nutty flavour, and is delicious raw or lightly steamed.

THE SITE

To grow well, cauliflower requires the soil to be at a pH of at least 6.5, but it grows best and is most likely to be free of root diseases in a nearly neutral or slightly sweet soil that gives a reading of 6.8–7.2.

SOWING

Start plants indoors where you can provide a germination temperature of 21°C (70°F) or more and early growth temperatures of at least 16°C (60°F). Start in trays a month before the last frost date so the seedlings will be no more than four to five weeks old when they go into the garden. Move the seedlings from trays to

Sow & Grow

CAULIFLOWER

(Brassica oleracea)
Botrytis group
Cabbage family (Cruciferae)

SOWING

Seed depth: 6–13mm (¼–½in)
Germination soil temperature: 27°C (80°F)
Days to germination: 6
Sow indoors: 4–6 weeks before last frost
Sow outdoors: From last frost to late spring

GROWING

pH range: 6.5–7.5
Growing soil temperature: 16–21°C (60–70°F)

Spacing in beds: Staggered pattern, 37.5cm (15in), 3 rows to a bed
Watering: Moderate and even
Light: Best yields in full sun; tolerates light shade
Nutrient requirements: N=high; P=high; K=high
Rotation considerations: Precede with a nitrogen-fixing cover crop; avoid following cabbage family crops
Good companions: Beetroot, carrot, celery, cucumber, dill, dwarf bean, lettuce, mint, nasturtium, onion family, pea, potato, rosemary, sage, spinach
Bad companions: Climbing bean, strawberry
Seed longevity: 4 years
Seeds per gram: 300 (8,500 per oz)

5cm (2in) growing cells as soon as they can be handled. Moderate but even moisture is critical at this time. You can direct-sow seeds in mid-spring if you want early crops or in early summer for autumn crops.

Growing

Transplant four-week-old seedlings to the garden in spring, about the time of the last frost, after hardening outdoors for at least a week. Transplant the plants carefully, being sure not to damage roots.

Watering and fertilizing. Keep plants evenly watered throughout the growing period. Cauliflower is a heavy feeder and likes frequent waterings with compost 'tea' or another dilute organic feed.

Blanching. A technique used for white varieties, this limits the amount of light that reaches the developing head. The result is cauliflower with a nice, white colour, improved flavour, and none of the unappealing ricey texture that sometimes develops during hot weather. Even self-blanching varieties have the best flavour and colour if treated like this. It's time to blanch when the head is about 5–7.5cm (2–3in) wide. Fold some of the leaves over the head and secure them together at the top with rubber bands or twine.

Harvesting and Storing

After tying leaves for blanching, check heads daily for maturity. In warm weather, harvest heads about four days after tying; in cool weather, harvest after about ten days. Don't wait longer than these recommended times to harvest, as the head may rot.

Cauliflower is ready for harvest when the head is tight and fairly regular, and the curd has not begun to separate (a condition called 'riciness'). Purple types have a more irregular head and should be harvested when the curd looks like a tight bunch of broccoli.

You can store cauliflower in a cool place or the refrigerator for about a month, but it tastes much better if used soon after harvest.

Best Varieties

Cauliflower is sensitive to cold and hot weather so horticulturists have developed varieties that are both cold and heat tolerant. These are most likely to give a good quality crop.

Early Dawn, Andes, Snow Crown and **Fremont** are all varieties with both cold and heat tolerance.

Celery

Thoreau once said that if someone doesn't keep pace with his companions, perhaps he hears a different drummer. After growing celery for some years, I think celery walks to the beat of a very different drummer. It has the reputation of being fussy, but it isn't really. It's just different. And, once you take account of the differences, it's not difficult to grow and certainly a pleasure to eat.

SOWING

Start celery indoors at least eight weeks before the last frost date. Sow seeds on a potting mixture rich with organic matter and lightly cover with washed sand or potting mix. It's important to remember that celery seeds need light to germinate, so don't cover seeds very deeply. Moisten, cover with clear plastic, and place in a warm area with indirect light. For best germination, keep temperatures between 18–24°C (65–75°F). Germination may be

△ **Celebrating celery.** It's easy to overlook this familiar vegetable, but as long as you give it fertile conditions, it will reward you with a crisp, sweet harvest for many months.

erratic, but seedlings should begin to appear in about one week.

When the plants are up, remove the plastic cover and move the container into a warm, sunny place. Be sure to keep the soil moist. If the plants are not already in pots or growing cells, transplant when there are two true leaves.

Sow & Grow

CELERY
(Apium graveolens var. *dulce)*
Carrot family (Umbelliferae)

SOWING
Seed depth: Just cover
Germination soil temperature: 21°C (70°F)
Days to germination: 7
Sow indoors: 10 weeks before last frost
Sow outdoors: Not recommended

GROWING
pH range: 6.0–7.0
Growing soil temperature: 16–21°C (60–70°F)
Spacing in beds: 20cm (8in), 3 rows to a bed
Watering: Heavy and even
Light: Best yields in full sun, tolerates light shade
Nutrient requirements: N=high; P=high; K=high
Rotation considerations: Avoid following lettuce or cabbage
Good companions: Almost everything
Bad companions: Carrot, parsley, parsnip
Seed longevity: 3 years
Seeds per gram: 2,700 (76,000 seeds per oz)

GROWING

Plant outdoors only after day temperatures stay consistently above 13°C (55°F) and night temperatures above 4°C (40°F). Pre-warm the soil with plastic mulch for a week before planting, and cover plants with polytunnels for about a month after planting.

Fertilizing. The key to growing good celery is working plenty of organic matter into the soil. Celery has a small root system and grows best in soil rich in organic matter. Before planting, add plenty of compost or rotted manure to the bed. Add some compost to the planting hole at the time of transplanting, and liquid feed with an organic fertilizer throughout the growing season.

Weeding and watering. Because the roots are very near the surface, keep the patch weeded but do not cultivate deeply. Check soil moisture regularly and water as needed, but don't let the bed get soggy.

HARVESTING AND STORING

Begin harvesting stalks from the outside of the plants whenever they are big enough to suit you. You can harvest whole plants by cutting them at the soil line. Gather plants when you want to; even small ones taste good. Celery can survive light frost if covered.

For best flavour and longest storage, water plants the day before harvest. Celery will keep in the refrigerator for a couple of weeks, or longer in a cool, dark, damp place.

BEST VARIETIES

Utah 52-70 is a disease-tolerant variety and produces reliable crops of sturdy, flavourful stalks. Blanching improves its flavour.

Ventura is an early, disease-tolerant variety with an upright habit, strong stalks and a tender, sweet heart.

Celeriac: A Celery Relative

Celeriac (*Apium graveolens* var. *rapaceum*) is a close relative of celery – and with the same flavour – though not as fussy, and is grown for its roots rather than its stalks. Grow it following exactly the same procedures as you would for celery. Harvest after the first few light frosts in autumn.

To harvest, loosen the soil around each plant with a garden fork and lift the root free. Cut the tops 2.5–5cm (1–2in) above the root and store in a cool, damp place.

During the winter, plant a celeriac root in a large clay pot in damp sand. Place it in a sunny window at room temperature and keep the sand moist. In a while you'll have small celery-like stalks and leaves for salads all winter.

Spring Celery Bonus

Before the first hard frost in autumn, I dig up half a dozen plants and replant them in large plastic buckets (be sure to provide drainage holes). I place them in a cool, damp place and water them whenever they begin to droop. We enjoy crisp, tasty celery all winter long and into the spring.

Chinese Cabbage

This Asian cousin of domestic cabbages combines a mild cabbage flavour with the look and texture of romaine lettuce. Open-head types have leaves with a loose, lettucy look, while closed-head, or Napa, types have outer leaves that wrap neatly over the top of the slightly tighter head. Whatever shape your Chinese cabbage takes, all types taste good, with a mild, slightly pungent, spicy flavour.

△ **This beauty's more than skin deep.** As frivolous as this vegetable may appear, it's both easy to grow and versatile in the kitchen.

SOWING

In warm regions, sow two seeds each in 10cm (4in) pots in late winter; in cooler areas, sow seeds in mid-spring. After seedlings emerge, thin with floral shears to one plant per pot. I like to thin after the first true leaves appear, to be sure the seedling I choose is the stronger of the two.

Summer crops. Set plants in the garden about four weeks after the true leaves appear and night temperatures are consistently above 10°C (50°F). Don't be impatient and move this plant into the garden too early, as a week or more of nights when the temperature drops below this temperature can trigger the plant to bolt a few weeks later. Chinese cabbage is sensitive to

Sow & Grow

CHINESE CABBAGE

(Brassica rapa)
Pekinensis Group
Cabbage family (Cruciferae)

SOWING

Seed depth: 6–13mm (¼–½in)

Germination soil temperature: 24–27°C (75–80°F)

Days to germination: 7

Sow indoors: 4–6 weeks before last frost

Sow outdoors: 10–12 weeks before first frost for autumn crop

GROWING

pH range: 6.0–7.0

Growing soil temperature: 16–21°C (60–70°F)

Spacing in beds: 30–45cm (12–18in), depending on type

Watering: Moderate and even

Light: Full sun

Nutrient requirements: N=high; P=high; K=high

Rotation considerations: Avoid rotating with cabbage family crops

Good companions: Beetroot, lettuce, onion, radish, spinach

Bad companion: Tomato

Seed longevity: 3 years

Seeds per gram: 250 (7,000 seeds per oz)

transplanting, so set plants in the garden very carefully so roots are not damaged.

Autumn crops. Direct-sow about two months before the first frost. Open-head, lettuce-like types provide a good autumn harvest. Plant as a successor crop to peas or early beans, which leave behind a shot of nitrogen in the soil.

GROWING

Like many plants in the cabbage family, Chinese cabbage has a delicate and fairly shallow root system that grows quite close to the surface. To grow the best Chinese cabbage, follow these simple guidelines:

General care. Water evenly from transplant to harvest, cultivate lightly and carefully, mulch during warm weather, and keep weeds under control, especially when the plants are young.

Fertilizing. Chinese cabbage can grow large and has a big appetite for soil nutrients, particularly nitrogen. Mix in plenty of compost at planting and feed every two weeks with an organic liquid fertilizer.

BEST VARIETIES

For spring crops, it is very important to use a bolt-resistant variety such as Blues, Kasumi or Orient Express.

HARVESTING

As with cabbage, Chinese cabbage can be harvested as soon as the plants are large enough to use. Cut the entire plant at the base and remove the outer, or wrapper, leaves. Freshly

harvested heads of spring and autumn crops will keep for about a week in the refrigerator.

Chinese cabbage keeps for several weeks in the root cellar, providing tender, tasty leaves long after the garden has been put to bed for the year.

To store, wrap the cabbage in newspaper and place it on a shelf in the root cellar or other cool spot. Autumn crops tend to store better than spring crops.

Pak Choi

After you taste this delightful Chinese vegetable, you'll know that pak choi spells stir-fry. A relative of Chinese cabbage, it has a tidy rosette of upright grey-green leaves. The large, succulent leaf stems vary in colour from snow white to creamy green. Try these varieties:

Joi Choi, about 30–45cm (12–18in) tall with icy white leaf stems, tolerates cool weather and is slow to bolt.

Chinese Pak Choi. About 37.5cm (15in) tall, this variety is very easy to grow and has excellent flavour. Its leaf stems are pale green and hold wide, thick, shiny leaves.

Mei Qing Choi. This dwarf, or baby, pak choi has pastel green leaves and pale greenish white leaf bases. It tolerates heat and cold well, is slow to bolt, and has an enchanting flavour.

Throwaways

Remove Chinese cabbage roots from the garden and discard them; don't compost. Chinese cabbage is subject to the same root diseases as the rest of the cabbage family.

Cucumber

Cucumbers like to climb on things. They just can't help themselves; it is deeply embedded in their nature. Breeders have tried to mute this trait by developing bush cucumbers, but even the caged bird sings. Inside every cucumber, whether it be bush type or vine, the desire to climb remains very strong, and with good reason, as you'll soon find out if you grow your cucumbers on a frame. Frame-grown cucumbers are straighter, more uniform in shape, and less likely to rot or be eaten by slugs or other pests. They are also less likely to become overripe because they have been overlooked by other plants. You don't have to grow your cucumbers on a frame, but you'll get more and better-quality fruits if you do, and you'll also use less of your precious garden space.

△ **It's easy being green.** Cucumbers mature rapidly, and if you keep the vines picked, you'll be able to harvest them over a long season.

THE SITE

Despite the fact that they are not as big as marrows or pumpkins, cucumbers still use a lot of soil nutrients. You will find that your

---

Sow & Grow

CUCUMBER

(*Cucumis sativus*)
Cucumber family
(Cucurbitaceae)

SOWING

Seed depth: 13–25mm (½–1in)

Germination soil temperature: 27–35°C (80–95°F)

Days to germination: 3–4

Sow indoors: 3 weeks before last frost

Sow outdoors: After last frost

GROWING

pH range: 6.0–7.0

Growing soil temperature: 21–27°C (70–80°F)

Spacing in beds: *On frames,* 45cm (18in); *on ground,* 90cm (36in)

Watering: Moderate until flowering; heavy from flowering to harvest

Light: Full sun

Nutrient requirements: N=moderate; P=high; K=high

Rotation considerations: Avoid rotating with other cucumber family members

Good companions: Aubergine, broccoli, cabbage family, sweetcorn, dill, dwarf bean, lettuce, nasturtium, pea, radish, sunflower, tomato

Bad companions: Aromatic herbs, potato

Seed longevity: 5 years

Seeds per gram: 35 (1,000 seeds per oz)

yield will be higher and that your fruits will be better-tasting if you apply 2.5cm (1in) of compost to the bed and work it into the top few centimetres of soil before you begin planting.

SOWING

In cool regions, start the plants indoors rather than direct sowing. Cucumbers do not like to be transplanted, however, so handle them carefully when you put them into the ground. Sow three seeds to a 10cm (4in) pot, three to four weeks before your transplant date. Keep the soil moist and temperatures above 21°C (70°F) during the day and 16°C (60°F) at night. When the first set of true leaves appears, thin to one plant per pot by cutting out the extras with scissors. Transplant after all danger of frost is past and the soil has warmed to about 21°C (70°F). Set out the plants on a cloudy day or in the evening, being very careful not to disturb the roots.

You can direct-sow cucumbers if the soil is at least 21°C (70°F) and promises to stay at least at this temperature during the germination period. You should use low polytunnels to keep the soil warm.

△ **Growing up.** You'll get cleaner, straighter cucumbers if you grow them up a support, such as this A-frame.

GROWING

This is a genuine warm-season crop, very sensitive to frost at both ends of the growing season and demanding warmth from germination right the way through to harvest. But cucumbers also mature quickly, so they don't need a lot of care.

Liquid feed, or rake in a complete organic fertilizer such as fish, blood and bonemeal, every two weeks. Once flowers appear it is very important to maintain even soil moisture, or misshapen, poor-tasting fruits will result.

With guidance, cucumber vines climb pea netting on the same frame used for other vertical garden crops. You can also construct an A-frame like that shown below left, and cover it with netting or chicken wire to support the cukes. They can be pretty rampant.

HARVESTING AND STORING

You can harvest cucumbers whenever they are large enough to use, and most gardeners find smaller fruits tastier than big ones. Check the vines daily, as the fruits grow quickly. Be sure to harvest when the cucumber is still dark green all over. A yellowing at the blossom end indicates an overripe fruit that is past its prime.

Although you can store cucumbers in the refrigerator for a week or more, they're best eaten fresh.

◁ **Bigger isn't better.** The fruit on the right will be much tastier, crisper, and less seedy than the over-mature one on the left.

Dwarf Beans

Dwarf (bush) beans include favourites such as Italian flat pod, French and purple types. Add to this flageolet beans, butter beans, and broad beans, and that's a lot of beans to choose from! What makes the selection easier is knowing that wherever you live, there is a type of dwarf bean that will grow easily in your garden and taste delicious, and it will be good for you, too.

△ **Flower buddy.** Insect pests of various sorts are less likely to bother dwarf beans if you grow marigolds nearby.

THE SITE

Dwarf beans, unlike climbing beans, are determinate, which means they grow to a certain size, flower, fruit and stop growing. Because the best part of a dwarf bean harvest lasts only a few weeks, you'll enjoy more, and better-tasting, beans if you make small plantings every 10 days.

Sow & Grow

DWARF BEANS

(*Phaseolus vulgaris,
P. limensis, Vicia faba*)
Pea family (Leguminosae)

SOWING

Seed depth: 2.5cm (1in)

Germination soil temperature: 24–29°C (75–85°F)

Days to germination: 7–10

Sow indoors: Not recommended

Sow outdoors: When soil temperature reaches 16°C (60°F)

GROWING

pH range: 6.5–7.5

Growing soil temperature: 16–18°C (60–65°F)

Spacing in beds: 10cm (4in) between plants in rows across the bed 20cm (8in) apart

Watering: Low at planting, medium at flowering, heavy through harvest

Light: Full sun

Nutrient requirements: N=low; P=moderate; K=moderate

Rotation considerations: Because they get along with just about all vegetables except members of the onion family, dwarf beans can go almost anywhere and be followed by just about anything

Good companions: Aubergine, beetroot, cabbage, carrot, cauliflower, celeriac, celery, chard, cucumber, leek, marigold, parsnip, pea, potato, radish, rosemary, strawberry, sunflower, sweetcorn

Bad companions: Basil, fennel, kohlrabi, onion family

Seed longevity: 3 years

Seeds per gram: 3 (100 seeds per oz)

SOWING

Starting beans too early is not doing them a favour. Cold soil slows down their germination, makes the seedlings more susceptible to disease, and can cause so much damage to the plants that they never produce a good harvest. Be sure the seedbed is moist but not wet and then rake it smooth.

GROWING

Watering. Beans need just the right amount of water as they develop. Too little or too much slows or stops growth and makes the plants more susceptible to diseases and pests. Water plants lightly, but evenly and regularly, from germination to flowering. Increase the amount of water from flowering to the formation of the first pods. Increase watering again from beginning to end of harvest. Avoid overhead watering, which wets the leaves and can promote diseases such as bean rust. In arid regions, be sure to water well once flowers appear to help ensure a heavy crop.

Fertilizing. Beans, along with peas, alfalfa and some other plants, belong to a group called legumes. Legumes are special because they get much of their nitrogen through a partnership

△ **Bean there, done that.** Instead of sowing one big crop of beans, make several small plantings about 10 days apart. You'll have a continuous harvest of tender, fresh beans over most of the garden season.

with rhizobia bacteria, instead of relying on supplies in the soil. But it takes a little time after germination for the bacteria to become established on the roots of each plant, so for a few weeks beans need to get their nitrogen from the soil like other plants.

Fertilize young bean plants with a complete organic liquid fertilizer, every two weeks for the first six weeks, then once every three to four weeks.

Give Your Beans a Bacterial Boost

Beans and other legumes supply much of their own nitrogen needs through their relationship with certain bacteria that live in their roots. They are able to do a better job of this and produce heavier crops if the seeds are inoculated with rhizobia bacteria before sowing.

Simply put the black powder containing the bacteria (available from specialist seed suppliers) in a bag with the seeds. Shake the bag until the seeds are coated, then sow.

Vive la Différence!

French beans. These are the familiar green beans, which are eaten, pod and seeds, when they're young and tender.

Flageolet beans. When the seeds of some beans begin to swell, but are not completely mature and ready for drying, they make delicious eating shelled, fresh from the pod.

Haricot beans. These are among the best of all storage crops and are also highly nutritious. Haricot beans are a valuable ingredient in cold-weather soups, stews and casseroles.

HARVESTING FRENCH BEANS

The easiest time to mess up a bean crop is right at the end. Until harvest, all dwarf beans look and act much the same. It is when it's time to pick the pods that the differences between French, flageolet and haricot beans become most apparent and important.

For French beans to taste their best, they must be picked at the proper time. Beans that stay on the plant too long are much less tender and tasty. And if you leave them unpicked even longer, the plant will stop producing new beans.

The best indicator of when to harvest French beans is the diameter of a pod, rather than its length. Length can vary by variety, while pod diameter is related to the maturity of the developing seeds. French beans should be picked when they're very slender, about 3mm (⅛in) in diameter. Don't let them get tough and stringy. At times of peak harvest, this can mean picking them about every other day.

Wax beans. Pick this type of French bean when the pods are a little larger, 6–10mm (¼–½in) in

△ **Slim and fit for picking.** The two beans on the left are too large and will be tough. The two in the middle are at their peak, but those on the right are too young and will therefore lack flavour.

diameter, or about the thickness of a pencil. Again, pick regularly to ensure best quality.

BEST FRENCH BEAN VARIETIES

Nickel. A French-filet type with small, very tasty, tender pods on strong, upright plants, Nickel is more tolerant of unfavourable conditions than most.

Vernandon. A long, straight French-filet type, Vernandon has pods that are both tender and crisp.

Slenderette. Sweet and delicious French beans with no stringiness or toughness, Slenderettes are heavy bearers and the plants are resistant to many diseases.

Provider. This bean has been a favourite variety for decades, in part because the pods are sweet and meaty. But these disease-resistant plants also grow well in cool weather and poor soil.

Goldkist. With tender, clean, yellow pods, this wax bean has good disease resistance.

HARVESTING HARICOT BEANS

Grow haricot beans like other dwarf beans but harvest when the pods are completely mature and dry. Good air circulation is important so that the pods don't rot before they dry, so allow sufficient space between rows. If you have a run of rainy weather after the leaves have died and the pods have begun to dry, pull the plants and hang them by the roots in an open shed.

BEST HARICOT BEAN VARIETIES

Etna, Midnight Black Turtle, Jacob's Cattle, Speckled Yellow Eye, Maine Yellow Eye, Vermont Cranberry, Soldier, Black Coco, Andrew Kent.

HARVESTING FLAGEOLET BEANS

Dwarf flageolet beans are grown in the same way as French dwarf beans but harvested later, when the pods are swollen with plump, tender seeds. Some varieties, such as Tongue of Fire, can also be eaten young as French beans, and others, including Flambeau, can be used as haricot beans. In cool regions, flageolet beans can be used as a substitute for butter beans; they don't require as much hot weather, something gardeners at higher latitudes may have in short supply.

BEST FLAGEOLET BEAN VARIETIES

Flambeau, Flageolet Chevrier Vert, Borlotto, Etna, Tongue of Fire.

Pennies in the Sand

Collecting colourful haricot and flageolet beans from the remains of the dry pods (threshing) can be as much fun as finding pennies buried in a sandbox. We usually thresh by hand, shelling each pod and admiring the pretty colours of the beans. It's fun to do this on an early winter evening with a fire in the fireplace. After you thresh the beans, make sure they are thoroughly dry and then store them in airtight jars. You can try either of these threshing methods:

▶ Take a handful of dried plants and gently bang them on the inside of a clean, dry dustbin.

▶ Stuff the dried plants in a clean sack or old pillowcase and tread on it lightly, then pick the beans out of the litter.

Winning at Shell Games: Broad and Butter Beans

Broad beans, also called fava or horse beans, are distant relatives of French beans. They have pods that look like fuzzy butter beans. These meaty beans have long been a staple of European cuisine, from the Middle East to Italy to northern Europe. In cool regions, they are used as a substitute for butter beans.

Sow broad beans as soon as the soil can be worked. Sow 2.5–5cm (1–2in) deep and 15cm (6in) apart. Pinching back the top of the plant when the first pods begin to form usually gives more uniform, higher-quality beans. Harvest for shell beans when the pods are plump, usually when they're about 15cm (6in) long.

Caution: Some people are allergic to raw broad beans, so be sure to cook them before serving them.

Butter beans love long stretches of warm weather, a quality that makes them of questionable value for gardeners in cooler regions. In warm areas, however, butter beans prosper, yielding delectable, tasty beans that resemble the shop-bought kind in name only.

Butter beans need even warmer soil (18°C; 65°F) than other beans for germination, are sensitive to the lightest frosts, and need warm and dry weather throughout a long growing season. Sow them 2.5cm (1in) deep – slightly deeper in sandy soils – and 7.5–10cm (3–4in) apart. As with other beans, harvest often to increase yield.

Dwarf butter beans for cool areas include: Jackson Wonder, Eastland Baby and Packers.

Dwarf butter beans for warm areas include: Dixie Butterpea, Fordhook 242 and Burpee's Improved Bush Lima.

Garlic

I've heard it said that if when you enter a restaurant you can smell garlic cooking, it's a sure sign that the food's going to be good. For some cooks, all sauces, soups, and stews begin with the full, rich flavour of garlic. Fortunately, growing your own garlic is pretty easy to do.

△ **A garlic trio.** (A) *Stiff-neck garlic* has a single ring of cloves enclosing a stiff, central stem. (B) *Soft-neck garlic* is the kind generally sold in supermarkets; it's less hardy than stiff-neck and may not store as well, though this largely depends on the variety grown. (C) *Elephant garlic* produces a few very large cloves with a pleasing, mild flavour. In reality a type of leek, elephant garlic is less hardy than true garlic.

PLANTING

Garlic likes to grow in deep, fertile soil that is well drained but has plenty of organic matter. Keep the pH where most other vegetables prefer it – at about 6.5.

Plant garlic cloves in the autumn about a month or two before the soil is predicted to freeze. In cool climates this can be as early as mid-autumn; in warm regions, early winter. For your first planting, purchase cloves from a garden centre, if possible choosing a variety that is known to grow well locally, or via a mail-order catalogue. (In future years, you can use some of your harvest from the previous year's

crop.) Use only the larger cloves, which will produce larger bulbs, and eat the smaller ones.

After planting but before the ground freezes, mulch with a thick layer of straw or leaves to protect the bulbs and encourage worm activity, which helps keep the soil friable.

Sow & Grow

GARLIC

(Allium sativum)
Onion family (Liliaceae)

SOWING

Clove depth: 5cm (2in), with pointed end up

Germination soil temperature: 13°C (55°F)

Days to germination: Not applicable

Sow indoors: Not recommended

Plant outdoors: Late summer to autumn

GROWING

pH range: 6.0–7.0

Growing soil temperature: 3–24°C (55–75°F)

Spacing in beds: 15cm (6in)

Watering: Low

Light: Best yields in full sun; tolerates light shade

Nutrient requirements: N=moderate; P=moderate; K=moderate

Rotation considerations: Should not follow any onion family crop

Good companions: Beetroot, lettuce

Bad companions: Bean, pea

Seed longevity: Not applicable

Seeds per gram: Not applicable

GROWING

Birdhouse gourds are best grown on a strong support such as a sturdy fence or frame. A dried gourd doesn't weigh much, but a gourd on the vine is very heavy. You can also allow gourds to sprawl along the ground, but if you do so, mulch them with a bed of clean straw to minimize any discoloration.

We set floating plastic mulch over seedlings or transplants to protect them from insect pests and birds. In addition to providing pest protection, mulches also add warmth to encourage fast growth. After flowers appear, remove the plastic so that insects can pollinate the blossoms.

Water plants heavily from sowing to about a month before frost, then reduce moisture by about one-third. This helps prepare the fruits for drying.

HARVESTING AND DRYING

Harvest a gourd when it turns pale. Gently snip the stem, being careful to leave enough stem to use as a hanger. Handle carefully, as bruised fruits often rot instead of drying. Wash the gourds gently in a 9:1 solution of water and household bleach, which also helps prevent rot. Hang in a warm, dry place until the seeds rattle when you shake the fruit. This usually takes about three to four weeks.

△ **An invitation to pollinators.** If you use row covers to protect young gourd seedlings, be sure to remove them when the vines blossom, so that bees and other pollinators can move among the flowers.

Making a Gourd Birdhouse

When the gourd is completely dry, use a wire brush and sandpaper to clean the outside. Use an expansion bit to cut an entrance hole 5cm (2in) in diameter in the centre of the gourd. Then use a serrated knife to break up the pith and seeds inside the gourd, and remove all of this material. To protect the gourd from fungal moulds and rots, treat it with copper sulphate. (Caution: copper sulphate is toxic; handle with care.) Wearing rubber gloves, dissolve 680g (1½lb) copper sulphate in 28.5 litres (7½ gallons) of water. Soak the gourd in the copper sulphate solution for 15 minutes, and then allow the gourd to dry.

If you wish, add a metal or plastic semi-circular canopy, 6.5cm (2½in) wide and 15cm (6in) long, above the entrance hole. Attach with silicone filler.

Paint the outside with one coat of white oil-based primer and three coats of white enamel paint. This reflects heat and keeps the inside of the gourd cool.

To hang the gourd, drill two 6mm (¼in) diameter holes at the stem end and insert a 30cm (1ft) piece of rigid wire (for example, coat hanger wire) through the holes. Fasten as shown in the drawing above. Drill five 1cm (⅜in) holes in the gourd's bottom for drainage. Hang your gourd birdhouse from a tree branch or from wire suspended between two sturdy posts.

HERBS

A vegetable garden I visited one summer stays in my memory because of what was missing from it. It was a warm, pleasant day, brushed by a soft breeze, and all around me were beds of vegetables. The tomatoes were just beginning to ripen, and the spreading leaves of cabbage plants were open to the sky. It was a really beautiful garden, yet as I walked around the plantings, it felt as if something was missing, something whose absence made the entire scene incomplete. It was all the more a mystery to me, because this garden really looked terrific.

Later, in another garden, I realized what had been wrong. The second garden also had vigorous, healthy vegetables, but as I wandered about the plantings I saw other things as well. Butterflies passed by, bobbing on the breeze and settling on a cluster of chives or visiting dill blossoms. Honeybees and black-and-yellow bumblebees buzzed and danced among basil flowers. As I brushed by other plants, the air became filled with warm spicy smells. This garden was not only healthy, it seemed alive. What was missing from the first garden now became glaringly obvious – herbs.

Herbs have been a part of gardens for thousands of years, yet somewhere along the way, herbs and vegetables became separated from each other. Herbs were rounded up to grow in herb gardens, while vegetables were hustled off to vegetable gardens. And what a shame, because herbs such as dill, sage and basil, for instance, make perfect additions to the vegetable garden. Here's why.

In vegetable gardening generally, there are many cases of things that go well together in recipes also growing well together. So it is with many herbs and vegetables. For example, basil and tomatoes are natural companions in both the garden and the kitchen; they go together like peas and carrots. In the kitchen, basil adds

△ **A treat for the senses.** Aromatic and flowering herbs add beauty and fragrance to the vegetable garden, while attracting butterflies, bees and other beneficial insects.

a rich flavour to tomato-based pasta sauce, and it's spectacular with sliced tomatoes in a salad. In our garden, basil helps repel flies of all kinds, including aphids, a major pest of many plants, and mosquitoes, a major pest of gardeners. In addition, basil flowers attract bees and other pollinators to the garden, which can help to increase your yields of tomatoes and many other crops.

Herbs add enjoyment to vegetable gardening and add zest and aroma to the dishes you create from the vegetables you grow.

H

Basil

Basil makes the perfect partner for tomatoes, not only in the garden, where its strong scent may confuse predatory insect pests, but also chopped and sprinkled on thick slices of juicy tomatoes, still warm from the sun. Basil has become such a staple for us that we think of it more as a vegetable than as a herb.

SOWING AND GROWING

A true heat lover, basil is very sensitive even to light frosts and can be permanently set back by temperatures below 10°C (50°F). It matures quickly and can be direct-sown, but in cooler climates you will get a more reliable harvest if you start plants indoors two or three weeks before the last frost date.

Where temperatures justify it, sow the small seeds 5–7.5cm (2–3in) apart and cover them with about 3mm (¹/₈in) of soil. Thin to 10–20cm (4–8in); the plants provide their own living mulch when mature.

Basil needs warmth and full sunlight but is otherwise undemanding. A light feeder, it's unlikely to need supplementary feeding, provided the soil is reasonably fertile. It doesn't need a lot of water, but its roots are shallow, so don't let the soil dry out.

HARVESTING AND STORING

Harvest the flower buds before they open and the leaves any time they are large enough to use. Pinch out the growing point; this keeps the plant bushy and you can use the 'pinchings'. Harvest the whole plant before frost, preferably in the morning.

You can store fresh basil in a glass of water at room temperature. You can also freeze it, either made into pesto or whirled in a blender with enough water to make a thick sauce. It's a terrific, almost-fresh seasoning for winter soups, stews and pasta dishes.

◁ **Pinch me!**
To induce a full, bushy basil plant and increase yield, pinch or snip out the growing tips. The pinchings are also your first harvest. Bon appétit!

Sow & Grow

BASIL
(Ocimum basilicum)
Mint family (Labiatae)

SOWING
Seed depth: Just cover
Germination soil temperature: 24–29°C (75–85°F)
Days to germination: 5–10
Sow indoors: 4–6 weeks before last frost
Sow outdoors: In warm regions, spring to late summer

GROWING
pH range: 5.5–7.5
Growing soil temperature: 24–29°C (75–85°F)
Spacing in beds: 10–20cm (4–8in)
Watering: Light and even
Light: Full sun
Nutrient requirements: N=low; P=low; K=low
Rotation considerations: Avoid rotating with marjoram or oregano
Good companions: Pepper, tomato
Bad companions: Bean, cabbage, cucumber
Seed longevity: 5 years
Seeds per gram: 600 (17,000 seeds per oz)

Chives

Chives are perennials and very easy to grow, at home in a pot on the windowsill as much as in the garden. So what's the catch? Well, sometimes chives can get a little invasive, tossing their seeds around the garden. It's a minor fault, easily remedied by snipping the flowers before they set seed.

△ **Spring fling.** Chives are one of the earliest plants to appear in spring, a first-of-the-year treat.

PLANTING AND GROWING

Grown from seed, chives take about a year before they're large enough to harvest, so most people purchase plants. Plant in spring where plants can grow for at least three seasons undisturbed. After three years, divide the clump and replant or give away the extras.

Set your chive plants in soil that has been improved with compost or rotted manure; no other feeding is needed.

Chives makes an attractive edging in the flower or vegetable garden.

HARVESTING AND STORING

In cool climates, chives die back to the ground in winter, but in warm areas they can remain evergreen throughout the year. You can harvest the leaves whenever they are large enough. Use a pair of scissors to snip individual leaves. Alternatively you can give the entire clump a haircut. The flowers have a more pungent, oniony flavour than the leaves and should be gathered just as they open.

Use chives fresh in salads or blend snipped chives with sour cream, butter or cottage cheese for dips and spreads.

BEST VARIETIES

Fine Chives. The long, very slender leaves on this variety are more attractive than many other chive plants.

Purly. This variety has stout, strong leaves that grow quite straight and tall.

Sow & Grow

CHIVES
(Allium schoenoprasum)
Onion family (Liliaceae)

SOWING

Seed depth: Surface or just cover

Germination soil temperature: 16–29°C (60–85°F)

Days to germination: 7–14

Sow indoors: T*ransplanting to garden,* spring; *windowsill growing,* any time

Sow outdoors: Spring or autumn

GROWING

pH range: 6.0–7.0

Growing soil temperature: 13–21°C (55–70°F)

Spacing in beds: 15–20cm (6–8in)

Watering: Moderate

Light: Full sun to partial shade

Nutrient requirements: N=moderate; P= moderate; K=moderate

Rotation considerations: Do not follow or precede other onion family crops

Good companions: Carrot, tomato

Bad companions: Bean, pea

Seed longevity: 1–2 years

Seeds per gram: 700 (20,000 seeds per oz)

Coriander

Coriander is a delicious herb that is pretty easy to grow and adds zip to your recipes and aroma to your kitchen. In the UK it's just called coriander but in the US it has so many names it's a wonder it doesn't have a split personality. When the leaves are happily growing in the garden, it is known as Chinese parsley. When the leaves are harvested for salsas and salads, it may be called cilantro. And the seeds that are gathered for mildly spicy casseroles and baked dishes are called coriander.

◁ **A multi-talented herb.** Whether you use the fresh leaves, or save the spicy seeds, you'll find dozens of ways to enjoy this fast-growing plant.

SOWING AND GROWING

Before sowing, improve the soil with some compost or rotted manure. Both transplanting and dry soil can cause the plants to bolt, so direct-sow the seeds and mulch plantings to keep soil evenly moist. Avoid feeding. For a continuous supply of coriander, make successive sowings every three weeks from spring to late summer.

HARVESTING AND STORING

Leaves. Harvest the entire plant when it's about 20cm (8in) tall. When gathering coriander, remember to harvest only what you need. It should be used fresh, as it quickly loses much of its potent flavour when dried or stored for more than a few days in the refrigerator.

Seeds. Allow the plant to go to seed. The seedheads will turn yellowish, then yellowish brown when ripe. Snip them off, bunch them together, and put them head first into a brown paper bag. Close the bag and hang the bunch upside down in a warm, dry place. As the heads continue to ripen, the seeds will drop to the bottom of the bag, where they can be gathered. Clean the seeds of any sticks or other debris and store in a glass jar.

Sow & Grow

CORIANDER
(Coriandrum sativum)
Carrot family (Umbelliferae)

SOWING
Seed depth: 6–13mm (¼–½in)

Germination soil temperature: 13–18°C (55–65°F)

Days to germination: 7–10

Sow indoors: Not recommended; does not transplant well

Sow outdoors: *In cool areas,* after last frost and every 3 weeks until autumn; *in warm areas,* autumn

GROWING
pH range: 6.0–7.0

Growing soil temperature: 50–75°F (10–24°C)

Spacing in beds: 15–20cm (6–8in)

Watering: Moderate

Light: *For seeds,* full sun; *for leaves,* light shade

Nutrient requirements: N=low; P=low; K=low

Rotation considerations: Avoid rotating with any other carrot family plants

Good companions: Tomato

Bad companions: Fennel

Seed longevity: 5 years

Seeds per gram: 140 (4,000 seeds per oz)

Dill

If dill's sole talent were flavouring pickles, that would be reason enough to include it in the garden. But of course pickles are just its opening act. Fresh dill leaves are essential to many seafood recipes, they're a great match for potatoes and onions, and they spruce up green beans and many other vegetables. And as if that weren't enough, dill attracts many types of beneficial insects to the garden.

SOWING AND GROWING

Dill is an independent plant that grows best if you leave it alone. If you fuss with dill, in fact, it won't grow well. As soon as you can start working the soil in spring, sprinkle dill seeds on the soil surface, and then pat them into the soil and water them. Once the plants are 7.5cm (3in) tall, add a layer of mulch to keep weeds down and conserve moisture. In many areas, dill readily self-sows.

HARVESTING AND STORING

Begin to gather the fresh leaves as soon as the plants are large enough. You can gather the flower umbels for pickles when most of the flowers are open. Harvest seeds when they turn from yellowish to brownish tan. Gather the seedheads and turn them upside down in a brown paper bag. Collect the seeds as they fall to the bottom of the bag.

BEST VARIETIES

Dukat. Slow to bolt, Dukat produces abundant, aromatic dark green leaves noted for their rich flavour.

Hercules. This dill produces very large quantites of ferny foliage.

Fernleaf. A dwarf form growing just 45cm (18in) tall, Fernleaf is perfect for small spaces and container gardens.

◁ **Another good garden friend.** Dill helps to attract many beneficial insects, including flies and predatory wasps. Interplant it freely in your garden to keep insect pests under control.

Sow & Grow

DILL

(Anethum graveolens)
Carrot family (Umbelliferae)

SOWING

Seed depth: Surface or just cover

Germination soil temperature: 16–21°C (60–70°F)

Days to germination: 7–21

Sow indoors: 4–6 weeks before planting out, but transplants poorly

Sow outdoors: *In cool regions,* every 3–4 weeks from early spring to midsummer; *in warm regions,* late summer into autumn

GROWING

pH range: 5.5–6.5

Growing soil temperature: 16–27°C (60–80°F)

Spacing in beds: 15–20cm (6–8in)

Watering: Heavy

Light: Full sun

Nutrient requirements: N=high; P=high; K=high

Rotation considerations: Follow beetroot

Good companions: Cabbage family plants

Bad companions: Carrot

Seed longevity: 5 years

Seeds per gram: 530 (15,000 seeds per oz)

Fennel

Have you ever met someone whom you got along with really well, but no one else did? Well, that's a good description of fennel. Gardeners love the stuff. Where fennel causes dissension however is in the garden. Most vegetable plants just don't grow well near it. The solution is a lot like when you have to deal with squabbling children: separation. It's a nice way to have your fennel and eat it, too.

◁ **Like having dessert for dinner.** Florence fennel has a sweet taste that makes any meal a really delicious treat.

SOWING AND GROWING

Florence fennel is a selected form of the species that forms a spreading bulb at the base of the plant, celery-like leafstalks, and ferny sprays of aromatic leaves. It's a plant with Mediterranean origins and likes warmth, so you should start it indoors about a month before the last frost. Fennel is best grown in a separate bed, so it doesn't disturb any nearby vegetables. It has few pests, though aphids may prove to be troublesome in some years. The plants usually require no feeding but need even, light watering for best growth, especially during dry times. Mulch around the base of the fennel plant to blanch the bulb and make it more tender.

HARVESTING

Harvest Florence fennel when the bulb is about 10cm (4in) across and firm to the touch. Collect the entire plant. The leaves can be used like sweet fennel. You should plan on using the stalks and bulb within a day or so of harvest for best flavour.

BEST VARIETIES

Zefa Fino has thick leafstalks and grapefruit-sized bulbs.

Rudy produces large, well-flavoured bulbs.

Sow & Grow

FENNEL
(Foeniculum vulgare)
Carrot family (Umbelliferae)

SOWING
Seed depth: 6mm (¼in)
Germination soil temperature: 18–24°C (65–75°F)
Days to germination: 7–14
Sow indoors: 4 weeks before last frost

GROWING
pH range: 6.0–7.0
Growing soil temperature: 18°–27°C (65–80°F)
Spacing in beds: 30cm (12in)
Watering: Moderate
Light: Full sun
Nutrient requirements: N=moderate; P=low; K=low
Rotation considerations: Avoid rotating with any members of the carrot family
Good companions: Fennel gets along well with mints and members of the mint family, such as sage, but that's about it
Bad companions: Just about everything
Seed longevity: 3–4 years
Seeds per gram: 250 (7,000 seeds per oz)

Marjoram

Marjoram's small green leaves, rising from a tangle of stems, have a unique fragrance, a blend of sweet and pleasantly pungent aromas that accents a wide array of dishes. Though not as easy to grow as its cousin oregano, it's not all that tricky if its few needs are met.

SOWING AND GROWING

Marjoram prefers a slightly acid to slightly alkaline soil with some compost or rotted manure added. It grows well in the company of cabbage family crops, such as broccoli and Brussels sprouts. Marjoram is a tender plant that does not like cold weather and has no tolerance for frost. In cool areas, sow seeds indoors a few weeks before the last frost; in warmer areas, you can sow directly in the garden after the last frost. Keep the soil evenly watered and mulch around the plants with a thin layer of straw.

HARVESTING AND STORING

You can begin harvesting the leaves when the plants are about 10–15cm (4–6in) tall. Gather individual leaves for immediate use or snip entire stems for drying and storage.

You can use the leaves fresh to season vegetable and pasta dishes. The volatile oils of marjoram dissipate quickly on cooking, so the leaves should be added to prepared dishes a few minutes before serving to preserve the herb's flavour. You can also dry marjoram and store it in jars for later use. It is one of the constituents of *herbes de Provence*.

BEST VARIETIES

Most seed companies don't sell named varieties of marjoram but instead offer the species. Here is one very nice exception:

Erfo produces an abundant crop of fragrant leaves on vigorous, upright plants.

◁ **Pot up some marjoram.** Enjoy plenty of marjoram fresh all year long, no matter where you live. Before the first autumn frost, dig up a plant and transplant it to a pot. Set the pot on a sunny windowsill away from draughts. You'll have aromatic leaves all winter.

Sow & Grow

MARJORAM
(Origanum majorana)
Mint family (Labiatae)

SOWING
Seed depth: Just cover
Germination soil temperature: 16°C (60°F)
Days to germination: 10–14
Sow indoors: 4 weeks before setting out
Sow outdoors: After last frost

GROWING
pH range: 6.5–7.5
Growing soil temperature: 13–27°C (55–80°F)
Spacing in beds: 15–20cm (6–8in)
Watering: Moderate
Light: Full sun
Nutrient requirements: N=low; P=low; K=low
Rotation considerations: Avoid rotating with oregano and basil
Good companions: Everything
Bad companions: Nothing
Seed longevity: 1 year
Seeds per gram: 4,250 (120,000 seeds per oz)

Oregano

Oregano is sometimes called wild marjoram, with emphasis on the wild. It's related to marjoram but has a bolder flavour as well as a hardier constitution – it survives as a perennial in temperatures way below freezing. And just taste how much zest it adds to your pasta and pizza sauces!

◁ **Early summer haircut.** Shear the plants about 5cm (2in) from the ground just before they flower in early summer. You'll have another harvest at the end of the season.

SOWING AND GROWING

You can grow oregano from seed, but many gardeners like to purchase plants so that they can sample the taste before the crop gets established in the garden. There's quite a bit of difference in flavour from variety to variety.

If you are going to grow oregano from seed, sow it indoors about two months before the last frost. As seedlings grow, select the most fragrant to transplant to the garden and put the remainder on the compost heap. Space plants about 30cm (1ft) apart in slightly acid to slightly alkaline soil. For the best-flavoured leaves, avoid feeding, do not overwater, and harvest before the plants flower.

HARVESTING AND STORING

You can harvest the leaves as soon as they are large enough to use. Pick individual leaves or snip entire sprigs. An alternative method is to shear the plants about 5cm (2in) from the ground just before flowering, and again about a month before the first frost. Use the leaves fresh or dry them and store in a jar for later use.

Not all Oreganos are Created Equal

Some oreganos are so mild they are of little use for seasoning. For the best, spiciest oregano, be sure to grow Greek (also called Italian) oregano. This plant bears white flowers and very aromatic leaves.

Sow & Grow

OREGANO

(Origanum vulgare subsp. *hirtum)*
Mint family (Labiatae)

SOWING

Seed depth: Just cover

Germination soil temperature: 16°C (60°F)

Days to germination: 7–14

Sow indoors: 8 weeks before last frost

Sow outdoors: 2 weeks before last frost

GROWING

pH range: 6.0–7.5

Growing soil temperature: 13–27°C (55–80°F)

Spacing in beds: 15–20cm (6–8in)

Watering: Low

Light: Full sun to partial shade

Nutrient requirements: N=low; P=low; K=low

Rotation considerations: Avoid rotating with marjoram and basil

Good companions: Everything

Bad companions: Nothing

Seed longevity: 1 year

Seeds per gram: 8,800 (250,000 seeds per oz)

Parsley

Mention parsley and for many people it will conjure up images of a token sprig of curly green leaves tossed on to the dinner plate for garnish only. This herb deserves much better. For starters, parsley is packed full of vitamin C, carotene, iron and chlorophyll. A single planting of parsley produces fresh leaves all summer and it is often the last plant still producing in the garden, even after a few light snows have fallen. You can also transfer a plant or two to a pot and bring it inside to sit in a sunny window to provide you with fresh seasonings all winter long. Parsley perks up any salad and adds its unique piquancy to everything from potato soup to meatballs and poultry stuffing. In short, parsley is not a one-trick pony, and once you start to experience and appreciate its many attributes you will probably want to grow more and more of it in your vegetable garden every year.

△ **Patience's reward.** Parsley may take a long time to germinate, but it repays you for the wait with beauty, nutrients and flavour.

Hurry up, Please, it's Time

You can either live with parsley's slow germination habit, or you can use one or more of the ruses gardeners have come up with to speed the process:

▶ Soak or refrigerate the seeds for a day before sowing them.

▶ Freeze the seeds, or soak them and then freeze them.

▶ Pour boiling water over the soil after you've planted the seeds.

Sow & Grow

PARSLEY
(Petroselinum crispum)
Carrot family (Umbelliferae)

SOWING
Seed depth: 6mm (¼in)
Germination soil temperature: 18–29°C (65–85°F)
Days to germination: 21
Sow indoors: Late winter to early spring
Sow outdoors: Early spring before last frost

GROWING
pH range: 6.0–7.0
Growing soil temperature: 6–18°C (60–65°F)
Spacing in beds: 15cm (6in)
Watering: Light
Light: Full sun to light shade
Nutrient requirements: N=moderate; P=moderate; K=moderate
Rotation considerations: Avoid rotating with carrots, celery, parsnip
Good companions: Asparagus, corn, pepper, tomato
Bad companions: None
Seed longevity: 1–3 years
Seeds per gram: 650 (18,000 seeds per oz)

Sowing and Growing

Parsley is not that fussy, but it does have one eccentricity – it takes three to four weeks to germinate. When other seedbeds are filled with seedlings, the parsley bed will still be empty. Just remember, it's nothing you did. That's just the way it is with parsley.

Sow parsley in fertile, slightly acid to slightly alkaline soil, and it will grow well. Parsley can stand a little shade, and it's a good companion to both tomatoes and asparagus, so it can be planted among either.

Parsley doesn't need a lot of water but does have shallow roots, so don't allow the soil surface to dry out.

Harvesting

Harvest as needed, beginning with the larger, outer leaves. To maintain production and quality, harvest the leaf stem along with the leaf blades. If you need a lot of parsley all at once, you can safely cut the whole plant, snipping the stems a little above the soil level. It will grow new foliage.

For fresh parsley all winter long, transplant one or two plants into 25cm (10in) pots in late autumn and then grow them in a sunny window. You can also start some seeds in a pot in late summer and grow the plants outside until the first frost of the autumn. Then bring them indoors.

Best Varieties

Two types of parsley are available through most garden centres, via mail order and from Internet sources.

Curly-leaved parsley has deeply curled leaves and a very attractive appearance. Its flavour is not as esteemed as that of the flat-leaved type, but it is still quite enjoyable. Varieties include Forest Green, with long, strong, nicely flavoured leaves that stay green even in hot weather; and Frisca, which produces very curly leaves that are equally attractive and delicious.

Flat-leaved parsley, also called Italian parsley, has flat, celery-like leaves. Gigante d'Italia has large, dark green leaves; the strong but pleasant-tasting leaves can be eaten fresh or added to recipes. Single-Leaf Italian bears leaves with a rich flavour, excellent for seasoning cooked dishes.

△ **Flat-out stronger.** Many cooks prefer Italian, or flat-leaved, parsley to curly, for its heartier taste.

Parsleyroot

All parsleys have roots, but only one type of parsley can be called parsleyroot. Although its leaves taste very good, parsleyroot (also called Hamburg parsley) is valued more for its large swollen root. It's about the size of a carrot and the colour of a parsnip, with a distinctive taste all its own. Grow parsleyroot the same way you grow parsley. To harvest, dig the roots, remove the tops, and store them in damp sand or sawdust, just like carrots. You can also leave them in the garden with a covering of mulch and dig them in spring like parsnips.

Grate parsleyroot raw into salads or coleslaw or serve it fried, baked, or boiled. For a winter treat, plant the root in a pot indoors and harvest the fresh sprouts all winter long.

Sage

Sage has a lingering, slightly spicy aroma that's as warm and inviting as a country kitchen when Sunday lunch is cooking. Generations ago, it was used to restore the body. Today, its fragrant bouquet instils a sense of calm and well-being, while adding beauty and fragrance to the garden. It is as pleasant a companion as any gardener could want.

PLANTING

Sage is a hardy perennial but quite slow-growing. Instead of starting plants from seed, you may want to buy year-old plants from a nursery or garden centre. This way, you'll get a fine harvest the same season, instead of the two growing seasons required if you start from seed.

GROWING

Sage prefers cool to warm temperatures and should be lightly shaded in very hot weather. Water plants during dry periods but avoid overwatering. Sage doesn't like wet feet, especially during the winter months.

HARVESTING

The leaves can be gathered at any time during the growing season. They seem to have most flavour just as the flowers begin to open. Purple-leaved varieties tend to be more aromatic than green-leaved types. Use the leaves fresh in recipes or add them sparingly to salads. You can also dry the leaves out and store them in airtight, dark-coloured jars for about a year.

BEST VARIETIES

Purpurea is a beautiful dusky purple in colour, with very aromatic leaves on an attractive spreading plant.

Tricolor has white, green, and purple leaves, making this variety particularly ornamental.

◁ **Looking good.** Sage adds grace and style to the garden while also repelling harmful pests.

Sow & Grow

SAGE
(Salvia officinalis)
Mint family (Labiatae)

SOWING
Seed depth: Surface or lightly cover
Germination soil temperature: 18–21°C (65–70°F)
Days to germination: 7–21
Sow indoors: 6–8 weeks before last frost
Sow outdoors: Not recommended

GROWING
pH range: 5.5–7.0
Growing soil temperature: 13–27°C (55–80°F)
Spacing in beds: 30–45cm (12–18in)
Watering: Light
Light: Full sun to part shade
Nutrient requirements: N=low; P=low; K=low
Rotation considerations: Plants should be replaced every 4–5 years. Avoid rotating with basil, cucumber, marjoram, oregano
Good companions: Broccoli, Brussels sprout, cabbage, carrot, cauliflower, kale, kohlrabi
Bad companions: Cucumber
Seed longevity: 2 years
Seeds per gram: 120 (3,400 per oz)

Tarragon

Tarragon is a traditional favourite in such French standards as béarnaise sauce and fines herbes (along with chervil, parsley and thyme). Its delightfully subtle, liquorice-like flavour is perfect with chicken and seafood. It's also a good for flavouring vinegars. A perennial herb, tarragon is easy to grow and hardy in most situations.

△ **Tarragon for the table.** Tarragon's narrow, shiny, dark green leaves pack a punch, with their combination peppery and liquorice-like flavour.

PLANTING AND GROWING

'A rose is a rose is a rose' may be true for that fragrant flower, but it isn't for tarragon. The most important thing to remember when you grow tarragon is to purchase the real thing. Lesson number one: don't purchase tarragon seed. French tarragon, which is the herb you need for cooking, is not propagated by seed but vegetatively, and is sold as plants. Lesson number two: purchase the most aromatic plants you can find. When you buy your plants, make sure the leaves are fragrant. Don't buy Russian tarragon, which does grow from seed but is bland and tasteless.

After you have bought your plants, set them in slightly acid to slightly alkaline soil. Avoid fertilizing and do not overwater them. Tarragon is amazingly drought tolerant. When the plants are three to five years old, remove them and replace them with new plants. You can also dig them up and cut off pieces of the roots to replant.

HARVESTING AND STORING

Gather the leaves to use fresh as soon as the plants are in full growth, about a month or two after they have been transplanted. The leaves are tastiest before the plants flower. Use them fresh in chicken and fish dishes, as well as with mushrooms, potatoes or leeks. Or steep tarragon leaves in white wine vinegar (about one part tarragon to two parts vinegar) for about four weeks.

Sow & Grow

TARRAGON

(Artemisia dracunculus var. sativa)
Sunflower family (Compositae)

SOWING
Seed depth: Not grown from seed

Germination soil temperature: Not grown from seed

Days to germination: Not grown from seed

Sow indoors: Not grown from seed

Transplant outdoors: Spring

GROWING
pH range: 5.5–7.0

Growing soil temperature: 10–27° C (50–80°F)

Spacing in beds: 30–45cm (12–18in)

Watering: Low

Light: Full sun

Nutrient requirements: N=low; P=low; K=low

Rotation considerations: Avoid rotating with sunflower family plants

Good companion: Basil

Bad companions: Artichoke, sunflower

Seed longevity: Not applicable

Seeds per ounce: Not applicable

Horseradish

Some people claim to grow horseradish, but this vegetable is so easy it really grows itself. Like asparagus, it's a perennial plant. Rather than growing from seed, it develops from pieces of roots called root cuttings. Just plant the cuttings and stand back. The first season, let the plants grow and develop a strong root system. Harvest the following autumn after the first hard frost.

△ **Caution: hot!** Horseradish is one of the few vegetables that come with a safety warning. Like hot peppers, it can be irritating to both your skin and eyes. When preparing horseradish sauce, work in a well-ventilated room or outdoors.

PLANTING AND GROWING

Although it demands little care, planting horseradish in well-drained, rich soil will provide a better yield. In spring, add some compost or well-rotted manure to the spot where you plan to grow horseradish. Loosen the soil with a fork to a depth of about 30cm (12in) as you mix in the compost or manure. After raking the bed smooth, dig a furrow about 15cm (6in) deep. Set horseradish root cuttings along the side of the trench so the buds are toward the soil surface. Cover roots with about 5cm (2in) of soil and water well.

The shoots should appear in about a week or two. After the first few leaves have completely unfolded, fertilize once a month with a complete organic liquid feed. Don't overdo it; horseradish doesn't need much help to grow quite vigorously. Water during dry spells.

HARVESTING AND STORING

After the first hard frost, loosen the soil around the plants with a garden fork. Lift the plants gently from the soil with the fork, trim off the tops, and brush the roots with a clean scrubbing brush to remove most of the soil. Remove some of the side shoots to replant. Store roots as you would carrots, in a cool, damp place, or in plastic vegetable bags in the refrigerator. Roots will remain fresh for about three months.

H

Sow & Grow

HORSERADISH
(Armoracia rusticana)
Tomato family (Solanaceae)

SOWING
Root cutting depth: 10cm (4in)
Soil temperature: 4–16°C (40–60°F)
Days to germination: Not applicable
Sow indoors: Not applicable
Transplant outdoors: Early spring

GROWING
pH range: 5.5–7.5
Soil temperature: 10–21°C (50–70°F)
Spacing in beds: 30–45cm (12–18in)
Watering: Low to moderate
Light: Shade to full sun
Nutrient requirements: N=low; P=low; K=low
Rotation considerations: Don't rotate
Good companions: Grow on its own
Bad companions: Grow on its own
Seed longevity: Not applicable
Seeds per gram: Not applicable

Jerusalem Artichokes

Because they spread rapidly, our 1.8m (6ft) Jerusalem artichokes grow in a special bed. Once shoots appear, a week or two after planting, the plants need little care.

PLANTING AND GROWING

Jerusalem artichokes grow from tubers rather than seeds. Each tuber (a swollen, knotty section of root) contains eyes, much like those of a potato. To prepare them for planting, cut the tubers into short sections; each piece must have at least two eyes. Don't allow the tubers to dry out.

Dig a trench about 15cm (6in) deep and sprinkle in 2.5–5cm (1–2in) of compost. Set the artichoke tubers on to the compost, spacing them 30–45cm (12–18in) apart. Cover and water well.

Keep weeds under control and water during dry periods. Apply an organic fertilizer once a month only where soils lack organic matter.

HARVESTING AND STORING

Although you can gather Jerusalem artichokes at any time from late summer to early winter, they taste best after a few hard frosts. After the plants have turned brown, cut back the stalks and loosen the ground with a fork. Use the fork to sift through the soil, gathering only as many tubers as you will use in the next couple of weeks.

Mulch the bed with a thick layer of straw to keep the soil from freezing so that you can dig tubers for many more weeks. Whatever is left in the ground will come up in spring and provide next year's crop.

BEST VARIETIES

Stampede produces large, white-fleshed tubers.
Boston Red produces tasty red-skinned tubers.

△ **Above and below.** Jerusalem artichokes produce small yellow sunflowers to lighten the spirit as well as tasty tubers that make dinner a feast. They are not related to globe artichokes.

Sow & Grow

JERUSALEM ARTICHOKES

(Helianthus tuberosus)
Sunflower family (Compositae)

SOWING

Tuber depth: 10cm (4in)
Soil temperature: 10–16°C (50–60°F)
Days to germination: 7–14
Sow indoors: Not applicable
Plant outdoors: After last frost

GROWING

pH range: 6.0–6.7
Soil temperature: 16–21°C (60–70°F)
Spacing in beds: 30–45cm (12–18in)
Watering: Moderate to heavy
Light: Full sun
Nutrient requirements: N=moderate; P=moderate; K=moderate
Rotation considerations: Don't rotate
Good companions: Grow on its own
Bad companions: Grow on its own
Seed longevity: Not applicable
Seeds per ounce: Not applicable

Kale

Gardeners, like parents, aren't supposed to have favourites among their vegetables, and I generally follow that rule faithfully. But if I did have a favourite vegetable, it would probably be kale. Kale is easy to grow and hardy enough to harvest even from under the snow. It can survive most winters without protection.

K

SOWING AND GROWING

Kale tastes best when it grows fast, so enrich the soil with compost at least a month before sowing. It needs cool, moist soil, so be sure to keep the soil well watered from germination to the end of the growing season. For better-flavoured leaves and less frost damage, stop watering after the first frost.

Though kale, like its cabbage relatives, is a heavy feeder, too much fertilizer is as detrimental to this plant as too little. Fertilize the planting every two or three weeks with a complete organic fertilizer such as fish emulsion. It is also important to keep the plants weeded.

HARVESTING AND STORING

The flavour of kale improves after the leaves are nipped by frost, but you can begin to harvest individual leaves as soon as they are large enough to toss in a salad. To avoid tearing the stems, use scissors or a sharp knife to gather the leaves. As the kale matures, you can harvest entire plants by cutting the stems about 2.5cm (1in) above the ground. Leaves stored in the refrigerator in a vegetable storage bag will remain in good condition for two weeks to about a month.

BEST VARIETIES

Low-growing varieties, such as Vates, are more frost-hardy than tall ones, such as Lancinato. But both types are equally delicious.

△ **Almost perfect.** Kale has just about everything – good looks, good flavour, good nutrients.

Sow & Grow

KALE
(Brassica oleracea)
Acephala group
Cabbage family (Cruciferae)

SOWING
Seed depth: 13mm (½in)
Soil temperature: 7–35°C (45–95°F)
Days to germination: 5–7
Sow indoors: 6 weeks before last frost
Sow outdoors: Mid- to late spring

GROWING
pH range: 6.0–7.0
Growing soil temperature: 60–65°F (16–18°C)
Spacing in beds: *Staggered pattern,* 40cm (16in) apart, 4 rows to a wide bed
Watering: Heavy during growing season
Light: Best in full sun; tolerates partial shade
Nutrient requirements: N=moderate; P=moderate; K=moderate
Rotation considerations: Avoid following cabbage family crops
Good companions: Beetroot, celery, cucumber, dwarf bean, lettuce, onion
Bad companions: Climbing bean, tomato
Seed longevity: 4 years
Seeds per gram: 350 (10,000 seeds per oz)

Kohlrabi

This fast-growing cousin of cabbage and broccoli is a very good vegetable to plant in late autumn, when garden spaces start opening up that would otherwise be wasted. The edible part of the kohlrabi plant is a swollen portion of the stem. It stores well in a cool, damp place and can be eaten raw or cooked in a variety of delicious recipes.

SOWING AND GROWING

If it is to be tender and tasty, kohlrabi must grow fast and without interruption. That means making sure it has rich, evenly moist soil and cool temperatures. Kohlrabi thrives on plenty of compost and benefits from leaf mould as a sidedressing. Start seeds indoors if you like, but best results come from direct-sowing. If you're growing kohlrabi as a late-season crop, start the plants elsewhere and transplant them as a succession crop when space is freed in the vegetable plot.

Once kohlrabi is off and growing, you just need to fertilize the plants every two to three weeks with a complete organic fertilizer and keep the soil moist. As the stems begin to swell, add a layer of compost or well-rotted manure to the rows.

HARVESTING AND STORING

To use kohlrabi fresh, begin harvesting when stems are about 5cm (2in) in diameter. Pull up the entire plant and trim off the leaves and roots. Store the plants in the refrigerator for a month or two.

For winter storage, harvest the stems when they have reached a diameter of 7.5–10cm (3–4in) after a few frosts. Trim the leaves and store in a root cellar for about three months.

In warm climates, kohlrabi can stay in the garden through autumn and be harvested as needed. If a cold snap is forecast, mulch the plants with straw.

◁ **The Eagle has landed.** Kohlrabi's unique growth habit makes the garden look like a moon landing site.

Sow & Grow

KOHLRABI

(Brassica oleracea)
Gongylodes group
Cabbage family (Cruciferae)

SOWING

Seed depth: 6–13mm (¼–½in)

Soil temperature: 10–21°C (50–70°F)

Days to germination: 5–7

Sow indoors: Not recommended

Sow outdoors: From early spring to late summer

GROWING

pH range: 6.0–7.0

Soil temperature: 10–18°C (50–65°F)

Spacing in beds: *staggered pattern,* 15–20cm (6–8in) apart, 4 rows to a wide bed

Watering: Moderate and even

Light: Best yield in full sun; tolerates light shade

Nutrient requirements: N=moderate; P=moderate; K=moderate

Rotation considerations: Avoid following cabbage family crops

Good companions: Beetroot, celery, cucumber, dwarf bean, lettuce, nasturtium, onion, potato, tomato

Bad companions: Climbing bean

Seed longevity: 3 years

Seeds per gram: 300 (9,000 seeds per oz)

Leeks

A bowl of leek and potato soup on a chilly autumn evening is all the reason I need to grow leeks in the garden. I know it's frowned on to personify vegetables, but leeks always seem friendly to me. They are gentle on the digestive system and they taste good, in addition to being easy to grow and frost hardy. They also stay fresh all winter long under a thick blanket of mulch. I know some people who don't have that many good attributes.

Sowing and Growing

Start long-season leeks indoors in late winter. Sow seeds in trays and, when the seedlings are about 5cm (2in) tall, transplant them to individual growing cells. Fertilize once every two weeks with a liquid feed.

△ **The short and long of it.** You can choose between short- and long-season leeks. Short-seasons have a thinner stem and don't keep as well as the hardier long-season types. I grow only long-season varieties like those shown above, with their thick, cylindrical stems carrying a fan of dark green leaves.

Sow & Grow

LEEKS
(Allium ampeloprasum)
Porrum group
Onion family (Liliaceae)

SOWING
Seed depth: 6mm (¼in)
Soil temperature: 24°C (75°F)
Days to germination: 5–7
Sow indoors: 4 weeks before last frost
Sow outdoors: Not recommended

GROWING
pH range: 6.0–7.5
Soil temperature: 16°C (60°F)
Spacing in beds: 15cm (6in) in rows, 3 rows to a bed
Watering: Moderate
Light: Full sun gives best yields, but tolerates partial shade
Nutrient requirements: N=moderate; P=moderate; K=moderate
Rotation considerations: Avoid following onion, shallot, garlic, chives
Good companions: Beetroot, carrot, celeriac, celery, dwarf bean, garlic, onion, parsley, tomato
Bad companions: Bean, pea
Seed longevity: 2 years
Seeds per gram: 350 (10,000 seeds per oz)

L

When they're ready for transplanting to the garden, about a week after the last frost, the plants should be as thick as a pencil and 15–30cm (6–12in) tall. Don't worry if they're bigger than that. With leeks, bigger transplants means bigger yields.

Leeks grow best in very fertile, well-drained soil, so add plenty of compost to the bed. Set the transplants as shown in the photos below.

Water transplants and then water regularly throughout the growing season to keep the stems tender. Fertilize them every two weeks with a complete organic liquid feed.

HARVESTING AND STORING

Harvest short-season leeks during the summer and long-season varieties from late summer through winter. To harvest, loosen the soil gently with a garden fork and pull the plants from the ground. Leeks don't store very long – about a week in the refrigerator – so harvest only as many as you need. In early autumn, but before the first hard freeze, mulch the bed with a thick layer of straw. This will keep the soil workable through most of winter, allowing you to harvest fresh leeks from the garden any time a craving for them strikes.

Transplanting Leek Seedlings

1 Remove the leek seedlings from the growing tray, gently teasing the roots apart with your fingers.

2 Trim the roots to about 5cm (2in).

3 Dig a trench about 20cm (8in) deep with a hoe. Set the leeks in the trench, about 15cm (6in) apart. Fill the trench with soil and press it down firmly but gently.

4 Mulch the planting with grass clippings.

5 As the leeks grow, mound the soil up around their bases. This traditional technique blanches, and sweetens, the stems.

Lettuce

People who aren't excited about growing lettuce should take a look at a garden full of today's vibrant cultivars or taste a salad made from the most interesting varieties. You can choose from hundreds of different varieties of lettuce in a wide range of shapes, colours and forms, not to mention tastes. Some of the different types include leaf lettuces, oakleaf lettuces, summer crisps, icebergs, romaines (cos), butterheads and bibbs. Grow a selection of lettuces, and your garden will be prettier and your salads taste better than you ever imagined. The secret to the sweetest lettuce is to keep it growing fast.

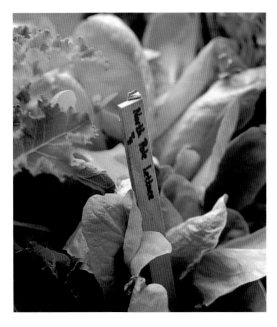

△ **Lovely lettuce.** This leaf lettuce, North Pole, flourished in our unheated greenhouse over winter, surviving outside temperatures of –29°C (–20°F).

Sow & Grow

LETTUCE
(Lactuca sativa)
Sunflower family (Compositae)

SOWING
Seed depth: 6–13mm (¼–½in)

Soil temperature: 4–16°C (40–60°F); germination rates decline above 20°C (68°F)

Days to germination: 7–14

Sow indoors: 4 weeks before transplanting

Sow outdoors: When soil can be worked

GROWING
pH range: 6.5–7.0

Soil temperature: 13–18°C (55–65°F)

Spacing in beds: *Leaf lettuce for continuous harvest,* 1.3cm (½in) in bands; *leaf lettuce to form heads,* 20cm (8in); *summer crisp and iceberg types,* 20–30cm (8–12in); *romaine (cos),* 25cm (10in); *butterhead,* 20–25cm (8–10in); *bibb,* 15–20cm (6–8in)

Watering: Light to moderate

Light: Full sun for best yields, but will tolerate partial shade

Nutrient requirements: N=high; P=high; K=high

Rotation considerations: Avoid following radicchio, endive, escarole, artichoke

Good companions: Everything, but especially carrot, garlic, onion and radish

Bad companions: None

Seed longevity: 1 year

Seeds per gram: 900 (26,000 seeds per oz)

SOWING

All lettuces are easy to grow and have similar needs although there are some important differences. Lettuces that form a head, including romaines, need more space to grow than leaf types. Some types, particularly romaine lettuces, tolerate warm weather better and are less likely to bolt.

You can start lettuce indoors or in a cold frame, or direct-sow it. If you choose to start the plants indoors or in a cold frame, sow the seeds about four weeks before you need to begin setting out. If you are direct-sowing seeds you can begin in early spring and continue through to late summer.

> ### Succession Success
> Lettuce is a good crop for succession planting. To have a continuous supply of lettuce over the season, make successive plantings every ten days to two weeks. As the weather warms, grow varieties that tolerate hot weather and resist bolting, such as crispheads.

△ **Getting big-headed.** Given space, butterhead lettuce forms a graceful, impressive head.

Lettuce seeds need light to germinate. Sow them on top of the soil and cover very lightly with soil. Keep the seedbed evenly moist. Lettuce germinates and grows best in cool weather. Although it's tolerant of light frosts, provide protection, such as a floating plastic mulch, if the temperature dips below −1°C (30°F). In warm soil, above about 24°C (75°F), the seeds become temporarily dormant.

GROWING

The key to tender and tasty lettuce is rapid growth, but lettuce has a relatively shallow, compact root system that doesn't absorb nutrients and moisture from the soil very efficiently, and this can slow growth. To encourage fast growth, add plenty of compost before planting, and again as a top dressing a week or so after seedlings appear or transplants are planted. Liquid feed with compost 'tea' every few weeks until harvest.

Lettuce doesn't require a lot of water, but it needs some water all the time. Lack of moisture causes plant growth to stop, which can also produce a slightly bitter flavour in the leaves. In warm weather, lettuce likes a little shade, which you can provide by growing it next to taller companion plants, such as climbing crops.

HARVESTING

Lettuce goes from seed to salad in about a month in many regions, and only a little longer in others. Once it has grown to the size you like best, there are three ways you can start harvesting the bounty.

Gather outer leaves. With all except the iceberg types, you can start gathering the outer leaves of your lettuces as soon as you feel they're big enough for the salad bowl. The harvest is over when a central stem starts to form. This signals that the plant is getting ready to bolt, and the leaves will start to have a bitter taste.

△ **A leaf at a time.** You can enjoy a continuous harvest of large outer leaves until the bitter centre core develops.

△ **A second chance.** If you cut leaf lettuce about 2.5cm (1in) above the soil, it will regrow one or two more heads.

Cut-and-come-again. Cut leaf lettuces about 2.5cm (1in) above the soil as soon as most of the leaves are salad-sized. The plant will continue to grow and provide a second and sometimes a third harvest.

Harvest the entire plant. This method is for all lettuce types. Wait until the plant is mature – but still young and tender – and harvest the whole thing.

STORING

If a crop doesn't store well in the refrigerator, that's usually viewed as a deficit, but I actually prefer lettuce straight from the garden. To get lettuce for a salad, I like to take an empty bowl out to the garden and enjoy the moments I spend gathering lettuce. When I'm done, I have a bowl of salad instead of just a salad bowl.

If circumstances prevent you from making daily jaunts to the lettuce patch, lettuce will keep for about a week in the refrigerator. Harvest in the early morning.

BEST VARIETIES

Leaf lettuce. In four to six weeks, leaf lettuce usually forms a loose rosette of tender, sweet leaves. Popular leaf lettuce varieties include Black Seeded Simpson, Simpson Elite, Red Sails, Red Salad Bowl, Impuls, Royal Oakleaf, Cocarde and Galactic.

Romaine (cos). Romaine lettuce has oblong leaves that form fairly loose, upright, conical heads. With a crisp, slightly tart flavour, it comes in shades of green and red. Varieties include Freckles, Romance, Rubens Romaine, Little Gem, Winter Density, Integrata Red, Rouge d'Hiver and Rosalita.

Butterhead and bibb. This is a very special class of lettuce that bears broad rosettes of tender, wavy leaves. The leaves have a delicate flavour and a creamy texture. Varieties include Sangria, Tom Thumb, Audran, Deer Tongue and Buttercrunch.

Summer crisp. This blend of some of the best features of leaf and head types results in a loose head of large, crisp leaves with good flavour. Varieties include Loma, Vanity, Sierra and Cerise.

Crisphead. Looking a little like an iceberg type and a little like romaine, crisphead lettuces produce large, crinkly leaves that have a crunchy texture and a pleasingly sharp flavour. They are all very heat tolerant. Varieties include Nevada, Micha, Cardinale and Canasta.

Melons

I think everyone who gardens has a pleasant memory of melons. Maybe this is because melons do best in hot summer weather – the kind of weather when outdoor picnics and get-togethers happen. Good times, good company, and good food topped off with slices of juicy melon! For me, every melon growing in the garden today carries something of all those summers from long ago inside it. All I have to do is cut a slice, take a bite, and the pleasant memories come back again.

There are lots of different kinds of melons – from muskmelons to watermelons. They are grown in very similar ways, but each has its own unique, enticing personality.

△ **Passport to summer.** A Galia-type melon, this Passport has sweet green flesh – a darker green near the rind fading to white-green at the centre. Because it's an early melon, it's a good one to grow in cooler regions.

Sow & Grow

MELONS

Cucumis melo
and Citrullus lanatus
Cucumber family (Cucurbitaceae)

SOWING

Seed depth: 13mm (½in)

Soil temperature: 27–32°C (80–90°F)

Days to germination: 3–5

Sow indoors: 3 weeks before last frost

Sow outdoors: When soil reaches 21°C (70°F) and after last frost

GROWING

pH range: 6.0–7.0 (6.0 is the absolute minimum; production drops below this)

Soil temperature: 21–29°C (70–85°F)

Spacing in beds: 40cm (16in)

Watering: Moderate and even from germination to hardening off; low for one week prior to transplanting; moderate again from transplanting until fruit is full-sized; low or none during ripening of fruit

Light: Full sun

Nutrient requirements: N=low; P=high; K=high

Rotation considerations: Avoid following cucumber, pumpkin, marrow, winter squash

Good companions: Sweetcorn

Bad companions: Potato

Seed longevity: 4–5 years

Seeds per gram: 10–35 (300–1,000 seeds per oz)

THE SITE

Melons are heat lovers. They really need more heat than they can get in cooler regions, but they can grow there with some help from plastic mulch and polytunnels. Melons are also a bit particular about pH, and their water needs fluctuate during the growth cycle. If you give melons the attention they need, however, they'll give you taste and sweetness you'll never get in a shop-bought fruit.

At the same time as you start the seeds indoors, work plenty of compost and some seaweed or rotted manure into the bed and then cover the soil with a sheet of black plastic to get it good and warm.

SOWING

Start melons indoors in seed compost, three weeks before the last frost date. Sow three seeds each in 7.5cm (3in) pots. Germinate the seeds at a steady 27–32°C (80–90°). Once the seedlings begin to appear, lower the temperature to 24°C (75°F) for about a week until the first true leaves begin to emerge. Using a pair of scissors, thin them to one plant per pot. Lower the temperature to 18–21°C (65–70°F) and then reduce the watering for another week.

Inside or Out?

In warm climates you can direct-sow melons, but starting plants indoors is preferred, both because the melon plants can grow well in soil 6–11°C (10–20°F) cooler than that needed for best germination of seed, and because the seeds germinate more slowly in cooler soil. Wherever you live, transplanting will probably give the best yields.

GROWING

Make sure the soil temperature is at least 21°C (70°F) before transplanting. Plant 40cm (16in) apart, one row in the middle of a narrow 75cm (30in) bed. To avoid transplant shock you need to be very careful not to disturb the roots while planting. In many regions, melons need every day of the growing season to ripen fruit and cannot afford any setbacks. After planting, cover the beds with floating plastic mulch to increase warmth and provide a barrier to pests. Remove the plastic mulch when the plants begin to bloom.

Melons are sensitive to drought throughout the season, but especially between the times

---

A Cantaloupe by Another Name

'Why can't melons get married? – Because they can't elope.' As common as this melon is, in some places what is called a cantaloupe is really something else entirely. In North America muskmelons are often called cantaloupes, but the two are actually completely different plants. A cantaloupe has a hard, warty rind, while a muskmelon, like the one pictured here, has a soft rind covered with netting. True cantaloupes (*Cucumis melo* var. *cantalupensis*) are rarely grown outside Europe.

of transplant and fruit set. To get fruits of the proper size, water evenly, but not too much, as excess moisture when fruits are enlarging can diminish flavour. Check soil moisture frequently. Fruits grow quickly and sometimes outgrow the nutrient reserve in the soil. Pale green leaves result. To correct this, use a complete organic fertilizer in liquid form, such as a seaweed formulation, from transplanting to fruit set.

△ **Fertilizer-wise tips.** From transplanting until flowers appear, use a fertilizer with more nitrogen than phosphorus or potassium, such as a 5-2-2. Later, from flowering until fruit reaches mature size, use a fertilizer with more phosphorus and potassium than nitrogen, such as a 3-5-5.

HARVESTING

It's pretty easy to tell when most vegetables are ripe, but with melons a little more practice is required to get it right. A nice tip to know is that all the fruits on any individual melon plant will ripen over a short period of time. If one melon is ripe, the remaining fruits won't be far behind.

Most melons. With the exception of watermelons and French Charentais, melons are ripe when the rind changes colour from grey-green to yellow-buff. The fruit is still firm, but gentle thumb pressure easily separates the stem from the vine.

Charentais melons. When the leaf nearest the fruit of these melons fades from green to pale yellow, you'll know they're ripe. Harvest charentais melons by cutting the stem (which is still firmly attached to the fruit) with scissors or shears.

Watermelon. Gauging when to pick a watermelon is bathed in as much tradition as science. Find the method that works in your garden and stick with it. The following are the most popular ways to determine when a watermelon is ripe:

▶ The tendril nearest to the fruit turns from green to brown.
▶ The underside of the melon, where it sits on the ground, is yellow.
▶ When you rap it lightly, you hear a low-pitched 'thunk' or 'thump' instead of a high-pitched 'ping'. Try a few that aren't ripe to tune your ear to the sound.

STORING

Store melons? Homegrown melons are too good to store. It's like asking children to save their Hallowe'en sweets for later. At harvest time the melons are lucky to make it from the garden into the house unscathed. But if you must pick and eat on separate days, all melons will store in the refrigerator for a week or so, and many melons taste even better chilled. It's your choice!

> ### It's in the Bag!
> If you have a place to train your melons up a strong fence or other sturdy framework, support the weight of the growing fruits by placing them in stretchable onion bags tied on to the structure.

BEST VARIETIES

Charentais. These produce medium-sized fruit with a greyish-green rind. The flesh is bright orange, intoxicatingly aromatic and sweet. Charentais melons are popular in France, but are becoming increasingly available elsewhere. Some nice varieties include Charmel, Alienor, Honey Girl Hybrid Charentais and Savor.

Galias. Galias bear medium to large fruits with greenish rinds covered with beige netting. The flesh is a translucent green that looks as refreshing as it tastes. The flavour is rich, sweet, and spicy. Some popular varieties include Galia Perfume Melon and Passport.

Honeydews. Medium melons with smooth yellowish white rinds, honeydews have flesh ranging from icy white to orange, depending on the variety. They are very juicy and nicely sweet. Some popular varieties include Earlidew, Hon-I-Dew and Honey Ice.

Crenshaws. These melons are similar to honeydews. Crenshaws produce medium to large fruits with a yellowish rind. The flesh is usually pale green in colour, but some varieties have an orange tone. Crenshaw varieties include Burpee Early Hybrid, Honeyshaw and Early Crenshaw.

Muskmelons. Medium to large, often ribbed, fruits that have rinds covered with tan netting. The flesh of muskmelons is sunset orange, juicy, and deliciously sweet. Some varieties are also nicely aromatic. Muskmelons are the most popular garden-grown melon. Some of the most popular varieties to choose from include Honey Bun Hybrid, Burpee Hybrid, Sweet 'n Early, Earlysweet, Ambrosia, Alaska and Earligold.

Watermelons. Popular everywhere, watermelons bear large to very large fruits with smooth rinds coloured from pale green to almost black. The fruit is so juicy it could come in a bottle, and it has that sweet, summery flavour that is, well, watermelon. There are many varieties, from the little icebox types favoured in cooler areas to the large arks grown in warmer regions. Here are some of the most popular: Yellow Doll, Sugar Baby, New Queen, Moon and Stars, Tiger Baby, Crimson Sweet, Sweet Favorite and Fordhook Hybrid.

△ **What a doll!** Watermelon doesn't have to be red. This Yellow Doll watermelon is even sweeter than the more common reds.

Okra

Okra is one of those plants that is as attractive as it is tasty. But beauty is much more than skin deep in the case of okra. In some parts of the world, where preparing and consuming the pods is an art, okra can be boiled, cooked slowly with tomatoes and spices, or dipped in batter, breaded and fried. It's a gem.

△ **Okra is more than OK.** Wherever you garden, easy-to-grow okra can add delicious variety to your garden and dinner plate.

SOWING AND GROWING

About three to four weeks before planting okra, warm the soil with black plastic. At the same time, sow seeds indoors in individual pots. After all danger of frost has passed, set plants 30cm (1ft) apart, being careful not to disturb the roots. In warm climates, you can also direct-sow okra.

Water plants during dry periods and fertilize once a month with a natural liquid fertilizer, such as a seaweed formulation.

HARVESTING AND STORING

Some people harvest okra pods when they are around 7.5cm (3in) long, but the pods are probably most tender and tasty if gathered when only 5cm (2in) long. Okra, like beans, is best when it's eaten the day it's picked. If this isn't possible, you can store it for a day or so in the refrigerator.

BEST VARIETIES

In recent years, a number of dwarf, spineless and early-maturing varieties have brought okra to short-season gardens for the first time

Cajun Delight is high yielding and crops early, making it the natural choice for gardeners in cooler climates.

Burgundy reaches 1.2m (4ft) tall with very attractive, deep wine-coloured stems and pods, as pretty on the plate as in the garden. The pods are equally tender picked large or small.

Sow & Grow

OKRA

(Abelmoschus esculentus)
Mallow family (Malvaceae)

SOWING

Seed depth: 19mm (¾in)

Germination soil temperature: 27–35°C (80–95°F)

Days to germination: 5–14

Sow indoors: 5 weeks before last frost

Sow outdoors: After last frost

GROWING

pH range: 6.0–8.0

Growing soil temperature: 21–32°C (70–90°F)

Spacing in beds: 30cm (12in)

Watering: Low

Light: Full sun

Nutrient requirements: N=moderate; P=moderate; K=moderate

Rotation considerations: Can be rotated with any other crop

Good companions: Aubergine, basil, pepper

Bad companions: None

Seed longevity: 2 years

Seeds per gram: 18 (500 per oz)

Onions

There's a story about a fellow who bought a dog in the hope of training her to watch over the house. But this dog had an independent personality, and the training went poorly. The more upset the owner got, the worse things became. Finally, he just gave up and let the dog do what she wanted to. As it turned out, the house suited the dog very well, and she became the best watchdog that anyone ever had.

Onions are a lot like that fellow's dog. To grow good onions, give them just what they need, and then don't bother them. Come harvest, you'll have a crop that will bring tears to your eyes.

△ **A harvest to cry for.** If you prepare the soil well but administer very little through-the-season care, onions are a satisfying crop to grow. This Stockton Red is a beautiful and colourful red onion.

THE SITE

Onions are finicky about certain things, and the soil they call home is one of them. The plants prefer fertile, loose, friable soil that is well drained with lots of organic matter. Sandy loams are just about ideal. Before planting, turn in good amounts of compost or well-rotted manure, no matter what kind of soil you have.

Sow & Grow

ONIONS
Onion family (Liliaceae)

SOWING
Seed depth: *For transplants,* 13mm (½in); *for sets,* 2.5cm (1in); *for seeds,* 6–13mm (¼–½in)
Soil temperature: 18–29°C (65–85°F)
Days to germination: 4–5
Sow indoors: 2 months before last frost
Sow outdoors: Spring

GROWING
pH range: 6.0–7.5
Soil temperature: 13–24°C (55–75°F)

Spacing in beds: 7.5–10cm (3–4in); for *spring onions,* 2.5cm (1in)
Watering: Medium and even
Light: Full sun for best yield, tolerates light shade
Nutrient requirements: N=moderate; P=moderate; K=moderate
Rotation considerations: Follow marrow or lettuce; do not follow any onion family crop or legume
Good companions: Beetroot, cabbage family, carrot, kohlrabi, early lettuce (in good soil), parsnip, pepper, spinach, strawberry, tomato, turnip
Bad companions: Asparagus, bean, pea, sage
Seed longevity: 1 year
Seeds per gram: 300 (8,500 seeds per oz)

SOWING AND PLANTING

You can grow onions from seeds sown indoors, direct-sow them in the garden, grow them from purchased plants, or grow them from sets.

Growing onions from seeds indoors. Onion plants grow very slowly and need a good head start on the growing season. About 8–10 weeks before the last frost date, sow seeds indoors, 6mm (¼in) deep, 13mm (½in) apart in trays or four or five seeds to a cell. Provide bottom heat and keep the soil moist. When the seedlings are tall enough for the tops to droop, give the plants a haircut (see below).

Direct-sowing onions. Because direct-sowing involves the least disturbance in the growth cycle, onions planted this way are less susceptible to stress and disease, less likely to bolt, and store better. Many onion varieties take a long time to mature, however, so direct-sowing may not always be the best choice in cooler regions.

In spring, when the soil temperature reaches 10°C (50°F), sow one to three seeds every 2.5cm (1in), 6–13mm (¼–½in) deep, in rows 10cm (4in) apart. When the seedlings are about 5cm (2in) tall, begin thinning. To produce onions to be used as spring onions, thin to 2.5cm (1in) apart. For the best overall yield, thin to 5cm (2in) apart. And for the largest bulbs, thin to 10cm (4in) apart. The thinnings can be transplanted, or you can toss them into spring salads.

Growing onions from purchased plants. Transplant purchased plants (as well as those you started indoors) to the garden four weeks before the last expected frost. For the best yield per square metre, set plants about 7.5–10cm (3–4in) apart in staggered rows. If purchased plants have long leaves, trim them back by about a third. Interplanting with a companion, such as beetroot, can help control weeds.

Planting onion sets. Commercial growers produce onion sets by sowing seeds very thickly and then growing the plants very close together. These crowded conditions make the plants mature rapidly, while keeping the bulbs small. This is important because by the time you buy the onion sets, they're already one year old and ready to flower (bolt), which you don't want them to do. Sets are more expensive than seed, but they are also a more reliable way of achieving a crop.

△ **Need a trim?** When seedling tops begin to droop, use shears to cut the plants back to about 7.5cm (3in) high. This stimulates additional root growth. Use the clippings in soups or salads.

△ **Smaller is better.** Small onion sets are less likely to bolt, so you should look for bulbs that are about the size of a five pence piece when you choose sets.

Plant sets 2.5cm (1in) deep, in a staggered spacing about 7.5–10cm (3–4in) apart, or in rows 15–20cm (6–8in) apart. If you grow both plants and sets, put them in different parts of the garden, as the sets are sometimes more prone to disease.

GROWING

Onions don't compete well with weeds and are easily damaged by weeding tools. Use regular, shallow cultivation to nip weeds early while avoiding damaging the onion roots.

Watering. Their shallow root system makes onions sensitive to fluctuations in soil moisture. Though plants don't need a lot of water, they like regular watering each week. Mulch to maintain soil moisture and control weeds.

Fertilizing. Onions don't require large amounts of nutrients, but their root system is so small and shallow they need to grow in highly fertile soil just to absorb what they do need. Topdress with compost in late spring. If needed, apply an organic liquid feed once a month. Be stingy, though. Too much nitrogen will produce lots of leaves and small bulbs.

HARVESTING

Onions are ready to harvest when most of the tops have fallen over. Just how many tops have to fall over before you begin to harvest is a moot point. In humid areas, wait until almost all the tops fall over. In drier areas, harvest the onion crop when about half the tops have fallen over.

Gently pull onions from the ground, and then leave them to cure in the sun for at least a week. When the tops and papery skin on the bulbs are dry and crinkly, clip the tops about 2.5cm (1in) from the bulbs and store in onion bags in a cool, dry place.

What is a Spring Onion?

A spring onion is any onion that produces a bulb no larger than the width of the base of the leaves. In garden catalogues, these are often called bunching onions. They have a softer, less penetrating flavour than onions proper. Some good varieties include Parade, Long White Tokyo, White Lisbon and Deep Purple.

Onions that are pulled before the bulb forms are also often called spring onions, although that's not what they really are.

◁ **Give your onions a sunbath.** When it is time to harvest your onions, try to anticipate a warm, dry, sunny spell so that the bulbs can cure in the sun for at least a week. If it rains, you should move the bulbs to an open shed or other covered but airy spot.

STORING

Not all onions store equally well. Sweet onions, such as Walla Walla Sweet, should be used within a few weeks of harvest. Onion varieties bred for storage, such as Copra and Prince, keep well for months. However, you should use storage onions grown from sets first, because they do not store as well as the ones grown from seed or plants.

Keep stored onions away from apples or tomatoes; these give off ethylene gas, which causes onions to sprout.

BEST VARIETIES

First Edition. This onion gives gardeners in cool regions all they want – full, rich flavour, long storage, and full-sized bulbs. The bulbs are tightly wrapped in bronze-copper skins that protect the pungent, juicy flesh. An excellent all-round onion.

Yellow Granex. This sweet, mild onion is extremely juicy but can be peeled with only the slightest hint of a tear. It is an excellent onion for hotter areas, where it will be properly pungent.

Stockton Red. Medium-sized, deep red bulbs have flesh that is mild enough for polite fresh eating, while still having real onion flavour. Stores well.

Walla Walla Sweet. This is a sweet, mild-flavoured onion that has been popular for over a century. It has juicy white flesh that is excellent in recipes that demand fresh onion. It does not store well.

Buffalo. If you prefer growing your onions from seed rather than buying plants, this one's for you. It produces medium-sized bulbs that have good onion flavour. Bulbs store for a few months.

Ailsa Craig Exhibition. These onions are big – very big. The large bulbs can be over 10cm (4in) in diameter, with ice-white flesh and just enough kick to let you know it's an onion. They are best used fresh but can be stored for a few months.

The Long and the Short of it

Onions are divided into two types, long day and short day.

Short-day varieties need about equal amounts of darkness and light to make bulbs, and grow best in warmer countries. One example is Yellow Granex, often called Vidalia.

Long-day varieties, which need about 14 hours of light and 10 of dark, are favoured in cooler countries. Long-day onions include First Edition and Baby Borettana.

△ **Practical and decorative.** If you plait your onion tops before they dry out, they'll store well and be a pleasure to look at as well.

Parsnips

Some people invest in the stock market; I invest in parsnips. This pale cousin of the carrot is like a bank certificate of deposit. I deposit some seeds and labour during the warm months, and my investment matures early the next spring, when my vegetable reserves are at their yearly low. A spring meal of parsnips freshly picked from the still-slumbering garden renews my energy and restores my faith that summer is just around the corner.

△ **Spring tonic.** To me, a true sign of spring is parsnips, sliced thinly and sautéed in a little butter.

SOWING AND GROWING

Parsnips can take even longer to germinate than carrots (about two to three weeks). Plant seeds 13mm (½in) deep and 2.5cm (1in) apart in rows 10–15cm (4–6in) apart across a bed. Keep the soil evenly moist during the germination period.

When the parsnips are about 10–15cm (4–6in) high, thin them to 7.5–10cm (3–4in) apart, apply a layer of leaf mould around the plants, and mulch with straw. That's it. Your part is done until harvest next spring.

HARVESTING AND STORING

You can harvest parsnips at the end of the growing season, but they don't develop their sweet, almost nutty flavour until after they've been through some hard frosts and preferably through a hard winter. Once you have lifted them, store them in the refrigerator or other cool place.

BEST VARIETIES

Harris Model. The snowy white flesh makes this parsnip very attractive, but its smooth texture and exquisite flavour are what make it exceptional.

Lancer. A Harris type with uniform roots, disease resistance, and excellent flavour.

Sow & Grow

PARSNIPS

(Pastinaca sativa)
Carrot family (Umbelliferae)

SOWING

Seed depth: 13mm (½in)

Soil temperature: 18–24°C (65–75°F)

Days to germination: 12–14

Sow indoors: Not recommended

Sow outdoors: As soon as soil can be worked

GROWING

pH range: 6.0–7.0

Soil temperature: 16–18°C (60–65°F)

Spacing in beds: 10cm (4in), in rows 10cm (4in) apart

Watering: Moderate

Light: Best yields in full sun; tolerates light shade

Nutrient requirements: N=high; P=low; K=low

Rotation considerations: Avoid following carrot, parsley, celery

Good companions: Dwarf bean, garlic, onion, pea, pepper, potato, radish

Bad companions: Caraway, carrot, celery

Seed longevity: 1 year

Seeds per gram: 240 (6,800 seeds per oz)

Peanuts

Everyone loves peanuts. The trouble is that the only peanuts we have are the ones for sale at the grocers. Peanuts don't like cold, but in warm parts of the world these relatives of peas and alfalfa are a standard part of the vegetable garden. You can choose from among four peanut types: Runner, a commercial type; Virginia, which has large kernels; Spanish, which are early maturers and therefore good in cooler climates; and Valencia, with sweet, small kernels.

SOWING AND GROWING

Before planting, work some compost or well-rotted manure into the soil. Peanuts do best in soils rich in calcium, so add lime (which also raises the pH) or calcium sulphate (which does not raise pH).

Sow seed peanuts in a hole 10cm (4in) deep or in a furrow about 5cm (2in) deep. As the seedlings grow, fill in around the base of the plants with loose soil. About a month after the stems emerge from the soil, blossoms develop near the bottom of the plant. When the petals fall off, the peg (the flower stem and peanut embryo), bends downward and grows into the loose soil. After all the pegs have buried themselves in the soil, mulch around the plants with a layer of straw.

HARVESTING

Two months after the plants flower, test for ripeness by lifting a plant with a garden fork. A ripe peanut will feel firm, with dry, papery outer skin. When the peanuts are ripe, lift plants from the ground with a fork and shake off excess soil. Cure the plants by laying them on netting in the sun for two or three days. Next, separate the peanuts from the plants and dry them in a warm, dry place for a further three weeks.

◁ **Surprise!** Growing peanuts is great fun. They grow underground, so you don't see your harvest until you dig them up. It's like waiting to open a present.

Sow & Grow

PEANUTS
(Arachis hypogaea)
Pea family (Leguminosae)

SOWING

Seed depth: 7.5–10cm (3–4in)

Germination soil temperature: 21°C (70°F)

Days to germination: 7–14

Sow indoors: 3 weeks before last frost, but difficult to transplant

Sow outdoors: After last frost

GROWING

pH range: 6.0–7.0

Growing soil temperature: 21–29°C (70–85°F)

Spacing in beds: 45cm (18in)

Watering: Heavy until peg enters soil; moderate thereafter

Light: Full sun

Nutrient requirements: N=low; P=moderate; K=moderate

Rotation considerations: Follow root crops such as carrot; avoid following legumes

Good companions: Beetroot, carrot

Bad companions: None

Seed longevity: 1–3 years

Seeds per gram: Not applicable

Peas

One of the nicest things about gardening is getting to know the vegetables you grow. Living in a world where most of our food is frozen or canned, we risk losing touch with what food looks like when it's growing. Vine-ripened tomatoes, fresh sweetcorn and tender, mouthwatering peas fresh from the garden are three of the best reasons for having a garden.

△ **Plan in autumn for next summer's crop of peas.** Since peas are one of the first crops to be sown in spring, you'll get the most from your pea crop if you get the soil ready for the spring planting in autumn by turning in lots of compost or rotted manure.

SOWING

Tradition holds that you should plant peas 'as soon as the soil can be worked', but peas germinate much more slowly in cold soil. And the colder the soil, the more slowly they germinate: from nine days in 16°C (60°F) soil, to 36 days in 4°C (40°F) soil. Let the soil warm up a little, helped perhaps by black plastic mulch. Peas planted a bit later catch up very quickly with those planted earlier.

Ask a bunch of gardeners about how far apart to space pea seeds, and you'll hear everything from 1.3–10cm (½–4in). I've had good results with very close spacing, about 2.5cm (1in), staggered in narrow bands on both sides of a frame. You can dip the seeds in an inoculative

Sow & Grow

PEAS

(*Pisum sativum,*
P. s. var. *macrocarpon*)
Pea family (Leguminosae)

SOWING

Seed depth: 2.5cm (1in)

Soil temperature: 4–24°C (40–75°F); the optimum is 24°C (75°F)

Days to germination: 14

Sow indoors: Not recommended

Sow outdoors: As soon as soil can be worked; late summer for autumn crop

GROWING

pH range: 6.0–7.0

Soil temperature: 16–18°C (60–65°F)

Spacing in beds: 2.5cm (1in), in a staggered pattern

Watering: Moderate until flowering, then low

Light: Best yield in full sun; tolerates partial shade

Nutrient requirements: N=low; P=low; K–low

Rotation considerations: Follow with kale

Good companions: Aubergine, carrot, celery, chicory, cucumber, parsley, early potato, radish, spinach, strawberry, sweetcorn, sweet pepper, turnip

Bad companions: Onion, late potato

Seed longevity: 3 years

Seeds per gram: 10 (200 seeds per oz)

solution before sowing, to be sure that nitrogen-fixing bacteria will be present in the soil.

GROWING

You may hear that you needn't fertilize peas because they can get nitrogen from the air. As with much garden wisdom, this is almost correct. The truth is that the bacteria that provide peas with nitrogen don't do this trick at the drop of a hat; they take a few weeks to really get going. Meanwhile, the plant has to get its nitrogen from the soil like any other. To help at this stage, when seedlings are 5–10cm (2–4in) tall, fertilize them lightly with a complete organic fertilizer.

HARVESTING AND STORING

Like sweetcorn, peas are delightfully sweet if you pick them at the right time, but they turn starchy if you don't.

Garden peas. For best flavour and texture, pick garden peas when pods have filled out but aren't bulging around the peas. Pick all the large ones you missed earlier, too. Pods left too long on the vine are a signal to the plant to stop producing more peas.

Mangetout. Pick mangetout as soon as the pod reaches mature length but before the peas in the pod are very much developed. Check often: the just-right stage doesn't last more than a day or so.

Sugar snap. Thick, succulent pods hold a host of sweet peas. These taste best when both the pods and the peas are plump and the pods snap like a bean pod. If the pod is stringy, remove the 'string' by breaking off the tip and then pulling the string up the inside curve and down the outside of the pod.

BEST VARIETIES

Garden peas. Fine-flavoured varieties include Knight, with plentiful, very early pods on

△ **Mind your peas.** Picked at just the right time, before the peas in the pod have developed very much, mangetout are tender and sweet, but over-large pods are tough and stringy.

75cm (2½ft) tall vines; Lincoln, a reliable heirloom, bearing long, slender pods filled with sweet peas; Green Arrow, a high-yielding variety with well-flavoured peas on vines 0.9–1.2m (3–4ft) tall.

Mangetout. Some popular varieties include Corgi, with thin, sweet pods that taste good in stir-fries; Oregon Giant, with very large pods around sweet, tiny peas; and Norli, with high, early yields of sweet, well-flavoured pods.

Sugar snap. Look for Super Sugar Mel, the best of the sugar peas, with disease resistance, early and heavy yields, and long, sweet pods; and Super Sugar Snap, a tall, 1.8m (6ft) variety bearing high yields of sweet, fine-flavoured pods.

Peppers

Peppers are a vegetable that can warm you right to your bones, with flavours from sweet to very, very hot. They come in many colours, including green, red, yellow, brown, orange and even lavender and purple. Peppers also come in different shapes, from squarish blocks to long thin cones and cherrylike balls. Regardless of flavour, colour or size, all peppers are grown in pretty much the same way.

SOWING

Most of peppers' special needs have something to do with temperature. They are very sensitive to frost at either end of the growing cycle. They like relatively high temperatures for germination and for growth outdoors. But, oddly, they benefit greatly from a jolt of cold early in life after they germinate.

About eight weeks before the last frost, fill trays or growing cells with seed compost mix or sieved potting compost. Sow the seeds

△ **Pick a pint of pickled peppers.** If you've never eaten green peppers fresh from the garden, you'll be surprised at how crisp and tender this common vegetable can really be. Fresh, frozen, or pickled, garden peppers earn their garden space over and over.

Sow & Grow

PEPPERS
(Capsicum annuum)
Tomato family (Solanaceae)

SOWING
Seed depth: 6mm (¼in)
Soil temperature: 27–29°C (80–85°F)
Days to germination: 6–8
Sow indoors: 8 weeks before last frost
Sow outdoors: Not recommended

GROWING
pH range: 5.5–7.0 (best results may occur at the acid end of this range)

Soil temperature: 21–29°C (70–85°F)
Spacing in beds: 30cm (12in)
Watering: Moderate and even until fruit set; less as fruit matures
Light: Full sun
Nutrient requirements: N=high; P=high; K=high
Rotation considerations: Do not follow with tomatoes, aubergine, potatoes.
Good companions: Carrot, onion, parsnip, pea
Bad companions: Fennel, kohlrabi
Seed longevity: 2 years
Seeds per gram: 160 (4,500 seeds per oz)

6mm (¼in) deep and water well. Keep the soil warm, between 27–29°C (80–85°F). Warm temperatures are very important for quick germination. Temperatures below 27°C (80°F) slow germination, and this gets the plants off to a poor start.

For increased flower and fruit production, try to provide your peppers with the following temperatures: as soon as the first true leaves appear, transplant into 10cm (4in) pots and lower the soil temperature to 21°C (70°F); 16°C (60°F) at night. When the third set of true leaves appears, lower the night temperature to 13°C (55°F) for four weeks. Moving plants from the house to a cold frame should accomplish this. At the end of four weeks, grow the plants at 21°C (70°F) day and night until it's time to put them in the garden.

Light is also important after the true leaves appear and while strong root systems are developing. Sunlight, especially in higher latitudes, isn't sufficient. Use artificial light – grow lights if you have them – to provide up to 16 hours per day.

△ **A bit of a shiver does peppers good.** After a warm germination period, peppers benefit from being in the cold for about four weeks before spending the rest of their pre-garden stage in more moderate temperatures.

Sometimes pepper plants begin to form flower buds before the root system is big enough to support a large crop. Remove any blossoms that appear before transplanting time and for about a week afterwards.

GROWING

Peppers love heat, so don't rush them into the garden before the soil is thoroughly warm. Use black plastic mulch to warm the soil, and floating plastic mulch to warm the plants once you've put them out.

Plant in a staggered pattern, 30cm (12in) apart, three wide in a 90cm (36in) bed. Peppers like each other's company and grow best when close enough so the leaves of the mature plants are just touching. As my mother used to say, 'peppers like to hold hands.'

Keep the soil evenly moist and remove the floating mulch when flower buds appear or the air temperature exceeds 29°C (85°F).

HARVESTING AND STORING

You can harvest peppers when they're green, but most are completely ripe when they turn red. When you harvest your peppers is largely a matter of personal preference. Red sweet peppers (bell peppers) are sweeter than green sweet peppers. And red hot peppers are hotter than most green hot peppers. People who prefer their peppers green do get a slight advantage over those favouring the red variety: as long as you pick the fruits at the green stage instead of letting them ripen to red, the plant continues to set new fruits.

Once they are picked, red or green, peppers will keep in the refrigerator for about two weeks. We like to freeze them for spaghetti sauces and soups by slicing them and putting them in a plastic freezer container. It's also easy to dry red peppers: just lay them on a screen, or string them and hang them in a dry, airy spot. Dried peppers retain their characteristic flavour for about a year when stored in clean glass jars.

Best Varieties of Sweet Peppers

Ace. A bell type and undemanding, Ace produces bountiful, early crops of large, slightly conical fruits.

Ariane. Sunset on a pepper plant! Dutch-style peppers turn stunning orange when ripe.

Early Sunsation. This bright yellow bell pepper has excellent flavour.

Hungarian Sweet Banana. Long and thin-walled, this pepper bears yellow to orange, very tasty fruits.

Islander. A bell type that's as colourful as a pepper can get, Islander bears large, delicious, lavender-purple fruits.

Sweet Chocolate. If only it were true! This pepper is named for its deep brown skin colour, Sweet Chocolate is more tolerant of cool weather than most varieties and bears reliably large crops.

Yankee Bell. Bred for cooler climates, this pepper bears nice, big, blocky fruits.

Best Varieties of Hot Peppers

Anaheim. A chilli pepper with manners, this variety bears long fruit that is pleasingly mild, with only a hint of its hot pepper heritage.

△ **How sweet it is.** Peppers are delicious when green or red or in between, but the red ones are the sweetest.

Bulgarian Carrot. Bearing bright orange fruits 10cm (4in) long, Bulgarian Carrot peppers add warmth to any recipe.

Firenza Jalapeño. This is the plant to choose if you want large crops of thick-walled, tasty hot peppers.

Numex Joe E. Parker. Hot enough to add zest and mild enough to be invited back, Numex Joe E. Parker produces more and better-tasting peppers than most hot varieties.

Thai Dragon. One of the best varieties for Asian recipes, Thai Dragon bears lots of 7.5cm (3in) long peppers that are very hot.

That Warm Feeling Inside

For centuries all those who ate them knew that not all peppers were created equal. Some – known generally as chillis – were much hotter than others. Around 1912, an American chemist called Wilbur Scoville devised a rather complicated way to measure the 'heat' of hot peppers. Today we know that the spiciness of a pepper depends on how much capsaicin it contains. But in honour of his contribution to the welfare of chilli lovers, their heat is still measured in Scoville units. As a point of reference for understanding the following ranking, pure capsaicin is rated at 15,500,000 Scoville units.

Pepper Name	Scoville Units
Bell Pepper	0
Anaheim	500–2,500
Jalapeño	2,500–4,500
Serrano	7,000–25,000
Cayenne	30,000–50,000
Thai	70,000–100,000
Habañero	100,000–325,000
Red Savina Habañero	350,000–550,000

Potatoes

Commercial growers supply us with so many potatoes that they seem to be everywhere, from our dinner plates to supermarkets to fast-food restaurants. With such abundance, why allocate space in the garden to potatoes? The reason is simple: homegrown potatoes are delicious – much tastier than shop-bought. Plus, you can try potato varieties that commercial producers just don't grow at all.

△ **A rainbow of potatoes.** Not too long ago, garden catalogues carried just a couple of potato varieties. Well, things have changed. Today the selection is so diverse that gardeners can buy a rainbow of potatoes, from yellow to red to blue – and when you get to the end of the rainbow, gold.

PLANTING

It's an advantage to chit your seed potatoes. Place them in trays in a well-lit, cool but frost-free place a month or so before planting; the aim is to have sturdy sprouts about 2.5cm (1in) long. They should go into well-fed ground in early to mid-spring, once soil temperature has reached 6°C (43°F).

You'll find that some seed potatoes are larger than others. You can plant tubers the size of golf balls in the ground without first cutting them; larger ones need to be cut into sections. Whatever their size, seed potatoes need some preparation about two days before planting.

Preparing for planting. Cut large tubers into pieces about 4cm (1½in) inches thick. Make sure each piece contains at least two 'eyes'. The eyes should be just beginning to sprout, but

Sow & Grow

POTATOES

(Solanum tuberosum)
Tomato family (Solanaceae)

SOWING

Tuber depth: 7.5–10cm (3–4in)

Soil temperature: At least 7°C (45°F)

Plant tubers outdoors: 3 weeks before last frost

GROWING

pH range: 5.0–6.5

Soil temperature: 16–18°C (60–65°F)

Spacing in beds: 30cm (12in)

Watering: Moderate, particularly during tuber formation, which is signalled by the appearance of flowers

Light: Full sun for best yields; tolerates partial shade

Nutrient requirements: N=high; P=high; K=high

Rotation considerations: Do not follow with tomato family plants

Good companions: Cabbage family, dwarf bean, horseradish, marigold, parsnip, pea, sweetcorn

Bad companions: Cucumber, pumpkin, swede, squash family, sunflower, tomato, turnip

Seed longevity: Not applicable

Seeds per gram: Not applicable

not so much that a stem has formed. As a rule of thumb, each piece should weigh between 45–60g (1½–2oz). To heal the cut potatoes, place them in a well-ventilated area at about 13°C (55°F) for one or two days.

After healing, treat potatoes with a light dusting of agricultural sulphur to guard against fungal diseases and ward off pests (see photos below).

Traditional planting method. It's usual to plant potatoes about 30cm (12in) apart in a shallow trench about 7.5cm (3in) deep. When the plants are about 30cm (12in) tall, earth them up by drawing soil up around them with a hoe until just the top few centimetres of the plant poke out from the soil. Some gardeners earth up a second time two or three weeks later. This method keeps the potatoes from turning green, but it's time consuming and may increase the likelihood of problems with high soil temperature and low moisture.

△ **This amounts to a hill of potatoes.** When the plants are 30cm (12in) tall, draw the soil up round them so that just a few centimetres of the plants show above the soil.

△ **Potato prep.** (A) Cut large tubers into pieces 4cm (1½in) thick, and then let them heal in a cool place for a couple of days. (B) Toss the potatoes in a paper bag with a handful of agricultural sulphur before planting.

Mulch planting method. Growing potatoes under mulch regulates soil moisture and temperature, makes the potatoes easier to harvest, and is less work all round than the traditional method. Plant in trenches 7.5cm (3in) deep and 30cm (12in) apart. When plants are a few centimetres tall, apply 2.5cm (1in) of compost topped by a layer of straw so that about half to two-thirds of each plant is covered. As the plants grow, add more straw, keeping the mulch at least 15cm (6in) deep.

Potatoes have shallow roots 30–37.5cm (12–15in) and are very sensitive to changes in soil moisture during certain periods in their growth cycle. Be sure to keep the plants well watered from the time they flower until two weeks before harvest.

△ **Straw mulch technique.** Instead of earthing up potatoes with soil, some gardeners maintain a thick (15cm; 6in) straw mulch around their potato plants.

HARVESTING AND STORING

You can harvest some tender 'new' potatoes a couple of months after planting, either by pulling a plant or by feeling around and snitching one or two from each plant, leaving the rest undisturbed.

Harvest the main crop when the foliage dies back. With a garden fork or broadfork, gently loosen the soil and feel around for the tubers. This is easier on the hands and better for the potatoes if you let the soil dry out a bit before the harvest.

Brush dry soil gently from the tubers, but don't wash them. Cure for about two weeks at around 13°C (55°F) in humid conditions, and then store at about 4°C (40°F) in a root cellar. Do not store potatoes with apples.

△ **Hunting for treasure.** Harvesting vegetables is a joy whether you're picking sweetcorn or pulling carrots. But letting your hands swim around in the soil feeling for potatoes is just plain fun.

BEST VARIETIES

Kennebec. One of the most versatile varieties, Kennebec's well-formed, yellowish tubers have good flavour; it is disease resistant and stores well.

Yukon Gold. Vigorous plants produce large, fine-flavoured, yellow-fleshed tubers that store well.

Red Sun. The tubers of this high-yielding variety have bright red skin and smooth-textured flesh.

All Blue. Colourful and tasty, All Blue bears lots of potatoes, with indigo skin and blue and white flesh.

Giant Peanut Fingerling. If you want a change from fluffy, bland potatoes, try these fingerlings, which produce 10cm (4in) long, pale tubers with firm, white flesh and a good flavour.

Gold Rush. One of the best baking potatoes, it has a flaky texture and sweet-flavoured flesh.

Radishes

If your experience with this vegetable is limited to small red salad radishes, you're in for a pleasant surprise. All told, there are well over 200 varieties, including French radishes, daikon radishes and other specialities, in a surprising array of colours, including white, purple, black and even green. Raw, they can be eaten whole, sliced, diced or grated, or you can cook or pickle them. Most are best eaten fresh, but some can be stored for months in a cool place. Although growing radishes is very easy, to grow them well you have to grow them fast and harvest them fast.

SOWING AND GROWING

Radishes are particularly sensitive to any interruptions in their growth. Above all, you should not allow the soil to dry out at any time. They thrive in cool, moist soil that contains a lot of organic matter, with a pH of about 6.5, and a readily available supply of nutrients. Radishes do particularly well where fallen leaves have been worked into the soil the previous autumn.

Sow radishes wherever there is an empty space, from early spring until early summer and again in autumn. They make useful 'row markers' sown among slow-germinating crops such as carrots and parsnips. As you harvest the radishes, they leave behind loosened soil and space for other plants to grow.

HARVESTING AND STORING

Radishes are at their best for a very short time. If they're left in the ground too long, they develop a sharp taste and pithy texture, followed a day or so later by split roots. Harvest the whole crop when it matures and store the roots in the refrigerator until you are ready to eat them.

◁ **Radical radishes.** Pulling up the radish variety Easter Egg is as much fun as having a go in a lucky dip. Until you harvest this fast-growing crop, you never know which of a rainbow of vibrant colours hides under the moist spring soil.

Sow & Grow

RADISHES
(Raphanus sativus)
Cabbage family (Cruciferae)

SOWING
Seed depth: 13mm (½in)

Soil temperature: 7–32°C (45–90°F); the optimum is 29°C (85°F)

Days to germination: 4–12

Sow indoors: Not recommended

Sow outdoors: Early spring and autumn

GROWING
pH range: 6.0–7.0

Soil temperature: 16–18°C (60–65°F)

Spacing in beds: *Small types,* 2.5cm (1in); *large (storage),* sow 5cm (2in) apart, thin to 10–15cm (4–6in)

Watering: Even and moderate to heavy

Light: Best yields in full sun; will tolerate partial shade

Nutrient requirements: N=low; P=low; K=low

Rotation considerations: Precede with a legume cover crop

Good companions: Flavour is improved by interplanting with lettuce. Also good with bean, beetroot, carrot, nasturtium, parsnip, pea, spinach

Seed longevity: 4 years

Seeds per gram: 90 (2,500 per oz)

Rhubarb

Some people prefer rhubarb pie, some strawberry-rhubarb jam. I think both are delicious and excellent reasons why everyone should have a patch of rhubarb in the garden. Usually exiled to the edge of the garden, this perennial can go just about anywhere. Once it finds a place it likes, however, it doesn't like to leave, so plan carefully.

THE SITE

Rhubarb likes rich, slightly acid, fertile soil with lots of organic matter. You can purchase either root divisions or container-grown plants. Select a site in sun or light shade, and plant in early spring, a few weeks before the last frost. Plant divisions 45–60cm (18–24in) apart, with the buds about 5cm (2in) below the soil surface.

GROWING

Water well after planting and keep the soil moist throughout the growing season. Snip off any flower shoots as they appear. Once established, rhubarb plants grow rapidly and often become crowded within 5–10 years. To rejuvenate the plants, divide them in autumn by slicing the crown with a sharp shovel. Dig up and remove one portion of the plant, fill the hole with soil, and replant.

HARVESTING AND STORING

Avoid harvesting the first year after planting and take only a few stems the second year. From the third year on, you can harvest more or less all you want. Rhubarb is most tender and has best flavour in the spring.

BEST VARIETIES

Valentine and **Strawberry** are rhubarbs with especially vivid red colour.

Cherry Giant likes warmer weather than most other rhubarbs.

△ **It's time for pie!** To harvest rhubarb, grasp the stem near the base and pull up, giving the stem a twist as you pull. You can also cut the stem from the plant with a sharp knife. Trim away the base of the stem and the leaves.

Sow & Grow

RHUBARB
(Rheum x cultorum)
Buckwheat family (Polygonaceae)

SOWING
Root cutting depth: 2.5–7.5cm (1–3in)
Soil temperature: 4–16°C (40–60°F)
Plant outdoors: Early spring

GROWING
pH range: 5.5–6.5
Soil temperature: 4–24°C (40–75°F)
Spacing in beds: 60–90cm (24–36in)
Watering: Moderate and even
Light: Partial shade to full sun
Nutrient requirements: N=low; P=low; K=low
Rotation considerations: Perennial crop; don't rotate
Good companions: Not applicable
Bad companions: Not applicable
Seed longevity: Not applicable
Seeds per gram: Not applicable

SALAD LEAVES

Sometimes you just don't notice things. For instance, I'd seen and eaten garden leaves all my life. They mingled with other vegetables in salads or sat shoulder to shoulder with lettuce in the produce section of markets. They certainly were around, but didn't catch my attention. Then one spring I started growing them in my garden, and that's when I began to appreciate their individuality: the meaty tang of winter purslane (miner's lettuce), the pleasant sharpness of rocket, the mild spiciness of mizuna, and on and on. When I blended these with lettuce and various other leaves, I had to completely redefine my idea of salad. It was like eating spaghetti all your life and suddenly being shown the pasta aisle in the supermarket. What a nice surprise!

But variety and flavour weren't the only surprise leaves had in store for me. The greatest and most welcome came one bitterly cold winter morning after an evening snowfall. Some weeks before, I'd planted a selection of salad leaves in our small, unheated greenhouse in the garden. This little patch had supplied a regular harvest throughout the autumn, but I didn't expect the plants to last through really cold conditions. It was well below freezing that morning, yet when I stepped into the greenhouse, the greens still lived up to their name – they were green. Later that day, I snipped enough of them for a nice salad, then trudged back to the house through the snow.

Perhaps it's not absolutely correct to call that experience my very first impression of leaves, but it is certainly the one I remember most. And I relate it now so you can see how valuable these delicious plants are to any garden. They are easy to grow, nutritious, tasty, and surprisingly hardy. They can transform vegetable gardening from a seasonal pastime to a year-round pleasure for just about anyone.

△ **Gardening's superbowl.** A selection of leaves can provide bowls of delicious salads for months, from early spring to early winter.

Mesclun: A Salad in a Packet

Mesclun isn't one particular vegetable – it's a whole salad. More and more seed catalogues offer mesclun mixes, which include seeds for a variety of lettuces and salad leaves that grow well together and also taste good together. All the included varieties are easy to grow. Many catalogues offer two, three or more different mixes. Add some mystery to your garden by trying out several kinds.

Before sowing, shake the seed packet well to mix up the seeds. Either space seeds about 13mm (½in) apart in rows or broadcast them in a thin band. Cover seeds with about 3mm (⅛in) of fine soil. Moisten the soil and be sure to keep it moist until the seeds have germinated.

Harvest in 'cut-and-come-again' fashion at about three weeks by cutting the plants with scissors 13mm (½in) above the soil. Most of the plants will regrow.

S

Cress

The most popular forms of garden cress are broadleaf cress and curly cress. Broadleaf cress has flat, wavy-edged leaves, while curly cress has leaves resembling parsley. Both are almost embarrassingly easy to grow, with some varieties going from sowing to salad bowl in less than one month. Their peppery, tangy flavour adds a pleasant zing to salads all year round.

△ **Greens for your windowsill.** Cress grown in containers provides a taste of spring all winter long.

SOWING AND GROWING

If the meek are destined to inherit the Earth, then cress will certainly inherit the garden. This stuff will grow just about anywhere. You can grow cress indoors in a tray or flowerpot for sprouts any time of year. Just fill a tray with moist seed compost, sprinkle the seeds over the soil, and lightly cover with a little vermiculite or seed compost mix. The seedlings will emerge in as little as two days and can be harvested any time after the first true leaves begin to appear.

To grow outdoors, broadcast seeds in bands about 7.5cm (3in) wide down the bed. Space bands about 10cm (4in) apart. Sow every two weeks from early spring until the weather warms. Resume sowing when cool weather arrives in late summer or autumn. Sow every two weeks until mid- to late autumn. In warmer areas, sowing can continue through most of the winter months.

HARVESTING

When the plants are 5–7.5cm (2–3in) tall, harvest by cutting them at the soil line with sharp scissors. Under ideal conditions cress can be harvested in two to three weeks from sowing. If plants get too large, or if the weather warms, the leaves will develop an unappetizing bitterness. Remember that with cress, harvesting young pleases the tongue.

Sow & Grow

GARDEN CRESS

(Lepidum sativum)
Cabbage family (Cruciferae)

SOWING
Seed depth: Cover lightly
Germination soil temperature: 13–24°C (55–75°F)
Days to germination: 2–6
Sow indoors: Any time
Sow outdoors: Every 2 weeks from early to mid-spring, then every 2 weeks from late summer to mid-autumn

GROWING
pH range: 6.0–6.7
Growing soil temperature: 50–75°F (10–24°C)
Spacing in beds: 2.5–5cm (1–2in)
Watering: Moderate
Light: Full sun, but tolerates partial shade
Nutrient requirements: N=low; P=low; K=low
Rotation considerations: Do not precede or follow with cabbage family crops
Good companions: Beetroot, carrot, celery, chamomile, cucumber, dill, dwarf bean, lettuce, mint, nasturtium, onion family, potato, rosemary, sage, spinach, thyme
Bad companions: Climbing bean, strawberry
Seed longevity: 5 years
Seeds per gram: 350 (10,000 seeds per oz)

Endive

There are three different forms of endive. Curled, or frisée, has crinkly-edged leaves and a sharp, bitter taste. Broad-leaved escarole, or Batavian endive, is a hardier plant, which has flat, thicker leaves and a less bitter flavour and there is also Belgian endive (chicory). You take your pick.

△ **Get the best from bitters.** Endive becomes bitter in warm weather. Grow in spring or autumn, and harvest young in hot weather.

SOWING AND GROWING

For spring planting, sow all endive varieties as soon as the soil can be worked. Make successive plantings every three to four weeks until the weather warms. For the winter garden, sow about two months before the first frost in autumn. Plants grown in autumn and subjected to a few light frosts have a richer, less bitter flavour than spring-grown plants.

Water plants evenly and regularly to ensure that the leaves stay green and keep growing. If the ground freezes in winter, withhold water unless the top of the soil dries out, and then water only very lightly. Plants grown in soil with lots of organic matter, such as compost, usually require no supplementary feeding. In poorer soils, apply a liquid feed such as seaweed once a month.

HARVESTING AND STORING

Harvesting can begin as soon as the outer leaves are of usable size. Gather the leaves as needed, or cut the whole plant at soil level. The leaves are best fresh.

BEST VARIETIES

Coral. An early-maturing Batavian-type that produces a thick head of broad leaves, Coral is slow to bolt and well-flavoured.

Sinco. A very tasty Batavian-type, Sinco has crisp, full-flavoured leaves.

Taglio. This variety matures early and is nicely flavoured. It is tolerant of many conditions, from hot to cold and wet to dry.

Sow & Grow

ENDIVE
(Cichorium endivia)
Sunflower family (Compositae)

SOWING
Seed depth: 6mm (¼in)

Germination soil temperature: 16–18°C (60–65°F)

Days to germination: 5–7

Sow indoors: 8 weeks before last frost

Sow outdoors: Every 2 weeks from spring to early summer and from late summer to autumn

GROWING
pH range: 5.5–7.0

Growing soil temperature: 45–65°F (7–18°C)

Spacing in beds: 30cm (12in); *for self-blanching,* 20–25cm (8–10in)

Watering: Moderate; light to none when grown in cold frame over winter

Light: Full sun to partial shade

Nutrient requirements: N=moderate; P=moderate; K=moderate

Rotation considerations: Avoid following radicchio

Good companions: Non-heading salads

Bad companions: Radicchio

Seed longevity: 4–6 years

Seeds per gram: 600 (17,000 seeds per oz)

Mustard

Mention the word mustard and people usually think of the yellow stuff on hot dogs. It's true that mustard seed is the major ingredient in the condiment that bears its name, but this versatile plant has more than one way to please the palate. Mustard greens can add a new dimension to salads with their meaty, decidedly spicy leaves.

SOWING AND GROWING

Prepare the soil as you would do for cabbage, a near relative, adding compost or another form of organic matter and working it in well. Mustard is tolerant of some cold and can be sown a few weeks before the last frost. You can start plants indoors if you like, but direct-sown crops seem to establish themselves faster and grow more vigorously. The plants grow quickly, with most types ready to harvest about a month from sowing. For best flavour be sure to provide the plants with an even supply of moisture and adequate nutrients: potassium is especially important. Seaweed fertilizers work well, or else you can rake in some fish, blood and bonemeal.

HARVESTING AND STORING

Begin by gathering individual leaves after the plant has formed a rosette of leaves, usually when the plants are about 7.5–10cm (3–4in) tall. You can cut entire plants at any time after they reach about 10–15cm (4–6in) tall. If they are cut 2.5cm (1in) or so above soil level, the plants will regrow, though the resulting leaves will be of poorer quality and will often have a bitter taste.

If some plants bolt and go to seed, you can gather the brown pods and save the seed. Mix the seed with other sprouting seeds, such as radish, cauliflower, onion, broccoli and garden cress, and grow a healthy and tasty blend of winter sprouts.

◁ **Cutting the mustard.** Like other greens, mustard is tastiest when grown in cool weather.

Sow & Grow

MUSTARD
(Brassica juncea)
Cabbage family (Cruciferae)

SOWING
Seed depth: 6mm (¼in)

Germination soil temperature: 18–21°C (65–70°F)

Days to germination: 4–6

Sow indoors: 2 weeks before last frost

Sow outdoors: Every 3 weeks from spring to summer for early crop and from late summer to early autumn for autumn crop

GROWING
pH range: 5.5–7.0

Growing soil temperature: 50–70°F (10–21°C)

Spacing in beds: 15–37.5cm (6–15in)

Watering: Moderate

Light: Full sun to partial shade

Nutrient requirements: N=high; P=moderate; K=moderate

Rotation considerations: Do not follow or precede cabbage family crops

Good companions: Beetroot, carrot, celery, chamomile, cucumber, dill, dwarf bean, hyssop, lettuce, mint, nasturtium, onion family, potato, rosemary, sage, spinach, thyme

Bad companions: Climbing bean, strawberry

Seed longevity: 4 years

Seeds per gram: 500 (14,000 seeds per oz)

Radicchio

Radicchio is a type of chicory that adds a distinctive zippy flavour to salads. It has been popular in Italy for many years, but older varieties were fussy and demanding, not qualities gardeners seek out. New varieties are easy to grow, and the lettuce-like heads, boldly marked with deep red and snowy white, make both the garden bed and the salad plate look vibrant.

△ **The price is right.** Colourful, tart and slightly bitter, radicchio is often costly to buy. Grow your own, and you don't have to worry about the price.

SOWING AND GROWING

You can grow radicchio as a spring crop, but it often matures after the days have grown warm, which makes the leaves somewhat bitter. As an autumn and winter crop, however, radicchio is hard to beat. It tolerates cold and frost very well, and, if you grow it in a cold frame, you can harvest it all winter long in all but the coldest climates.

For autumn and winter crops, begin sowing in midsummer, with succession sowings every 10 to 14 days for a month. For spring crops, direct-sow in the garden as soon as the soil can be worked.

HARVESTING AND STORING

Unlike the old varieties of radicchio, the new varieties don't need to be cut back before the heads form. We harvest as soon as the heads are firm. Radicchio remains fresh in the refrigerator for a few days and holds in the garden equally long if the weather is cool.

BEST VARIETIES

Giulio. An excellent variety for spring crops, Giulio produces bright red heads about 90 days from sowing. It is vigorous, slow to bolt and delicious.

Augusto. One of the most cold-tolerant varieties available, Augusto is excellent for autumn and winter crops.

Sow & Grow

RADICCHIO
(Cichorium intybus)
Chicory family (Asteraceae)

SOWING
Seed depth: 6mm (¼in)
Germination soil temperature: 16–18°C (60–65°F)
Days to germination: 5–7
Sow indoors: 8 weeks before last frost
Sow outdoors: 2 weeks before last frost and 2 months before first autumn frost

GROWING
pH range: 5.5–6.8
Growing soil temperature: 7–18°C (45–65°F)
Spacing in beds: 20–25cm (8–10in)
Watering: Moderate; light to none over winter
Light: Full sun to partial shade
Nutrient requirements: N=moderate; P=moderate; K=moderate
Rotation considerations: Do not follow endive
Good companions: Lettuce
Bad companions: Endive
Seed longevity: 5 years
Seeds per gram: 530 (15,000 seeds per oz)

Red Orache

Orache, also known as mountain spinach, tastes a bit like real spinach. Yet, while it's easy to see the similarities, it is its differences from spinach that make orache such a special addition to the garden. There are three types – green, red, and gold – with the plant of each colour having a flavour and texture all its own. Grown together in a bed or tossed in a salad, the beauty of orache's emerald, burgundy and gold leaves is surpassed only by its flavour.

◁ **Seeing red.** Colourful in the garden and in the bowl, red orache is an excellent addition to your salad garden.

SOWING AND GROWING
Orache is a cool-weather green that is easy to grow in most fertile soils that contain some organic matter. Sow seeds every two weeks beginning in early spring and continuing until the weather starts to warm up. Orache tolerates warm weather but tastes best when temperatures are cool.

HARVESTING AND STORING
Begin harvesting the leaves for fresh salads when they are 2.5–4cm (1–1½in) long; if you would like to steam the leaves, harvest them when they are 7.5–10cm (3–4in) long. You can either gather the leaves individually until the plants begin to flower, or you can cut the entire plant at soil level when it reaches about 15cm (6in) tall.

BEST VARIETIES
Green orache, such as Green Spires, produces attractive green foliage with a balanced, slightly sweet flavour.

Red orache, including Rubra and Purple Savoyed, produces dark, wine-red leaves with a rich spinach-like taste.

Gold orache, such as Aureus, bears yellowish gold leaves with a softer flavour than either red or green orache.

Sow & Grow

RED ORACHE
(Atriplex hortensis)
Buckwheat family (Chenopodiaceae)

SOWING
Seed depth: 13mm (½in)
Germination soil temperature: 10–18°C (50–65°F)
Days to germination: 7–14
Sow indoors: 3 weeks before last frost
Sow outdoors: After soil reaches germination temperature

GROWING
pH range: 6.5–7.5
Growing soil temperature: 10–24°C (50–75°F)
Spacing in beds: 5cm (2in); thin to 15cm (6in)
Watering: Moderate
Light: Full sun to partial shade
Nutrient requirements: N=moderate; P=moderate; K=moderate
Rotation considerations: Do not follow or precede with beetroot, spinach, Swiss chard
Good companions: Cabbage family, celery, legumes, lettuce, onion, pea, radish, strawberry
Bad companions: Potato
Seed longevity: 5 years
Seeds per gram: 300 (9,000 seeds per oz)

Rocket

One of many salad leaves long popular in the Mediterranean but now widely grown and enjoyed in other parts of the world, rocket (arugula) adds a delightful nip to salads. Preferring cool weather, rocket is sufficiently frost hardy to survive right through winter in a cold frame or unheated greenhouse. The plant is small, with a compact root system, so it's easy to grow in containers or in a tray on a sunny windowsill.

SOWING AND GROWING

Prepare the seedbed by working some finished compost into the top 7.5cm (3in) of soil. Plant the seeds outdoors in spring as soon as the soil can be worked. Make additional plantings every three weeks as long as the cool weather lasts. For a winter harvest, sow the seeds in mid-autumn.

HARVESTING

You'll be able to begin harvesting rocket leaves when they're about 5–7.5cm (2–3in) long, two or three weeks after the plants germinate. Cut individual leaves or whole plants. The leaves are best when young, but they retain a good flavour until the plant starts to bolt. The small, dark-veined four-petalled flowers are also edible, so let some plants blossom, gather the flowers, and toss them in among the leaves of your salad.

BEST VARIETIES

Astro. This variety is ready to harvest a few days earlier than most others and also has a milder flavour.

Skyrocket. Another early variety, Skyrocket bears tender serrated leaves and has a spicy, peppery flavour.

Italian Wild Rustic. This old variety has tender leaves, a spicy flavour and excellent yields.

◁ **Très gourmet.** Tangy is the best way to describe the flavour of this easy-to-grow salad leaf.

Sow & Grow

ROCKET
(Eruca vesicaria)
Cabbage family (Cruciferae)

SOWING
Seed depth: 6mm (¼in)

Germination soil temperature: 4–13°C (40–55°F)

Days to germination: 5–7

Sow indoors: Late autumn through to early spring

Sow outdoors: As soon as soil can be worked

GROWING
pH range: 6.0–7.0

Growing soil temperature: 10–18°C (50–65°F)

Spacing in beds: *In rows,* 2.5cm (1in); *in beds,* 15cm (6in); thin progressively to 15cm (6in)

Watering: Moderate and even; light in cold frame

Light: Full sun to partial shade

Nutrient requirements: N=low; P=low; K=low

Rotation considerations: Avoid following plants of the cabbage family

Good companions: Beetroot, carrot, celery, cucumber, dill, dwarf bean, lettuce, onion family, potato, spinach

Bad companions: Climbing bean, strawberry

Seed longevity: 5 years

Seeds per gram: 530 (15,000 seeds per oz)

Winter Purslane

Winter purslane, also called miner's lettuce, isn't the best-known salad leaf, but it is certainly one of the best tasting and easiest to grow. Originally from North America but now found in the wild elsewhere, it has gone largely unnoticed by gardeners for years. This is a pity, because it's another in that wonderful group of cool-weather, frost-hardy leaves that can supply salads all winter from a cold frame or unheated greenhouse.

◁ **Cool-weather beauty.** Easy to grow, uniquely attractive, frost hardy and tasty to boot, winter purslane is a good leaf to get acquainted with.

SOWING AND GROWING

Winter purslane is as decorative as it is tasty. Perhaps because of its wild origins, it is also easy to raise and grows vigorously even during the colder months. Like other cool-weather leaves, it languishes in the heat of summer. Before planting, work at least 2.5cm (1in) of compost into the seedbed.

In cold areas, sow seeds in the garden every three weeks from early spring to mid-spring, then begin again in late summer to mid-autumn. For winter leaves, put the mid-autumn sowing in a cold frame or unheated greenhouse.

In warmer areas, make sowings in the garden in late autumn and successively every three weeks until early winter for winter and early spring crops.

HARVESTING

Begin harvesting as soon as leaves are of edible size. If you cut individual leaves and stems as they are needed, the plant will continue to grow and produce. If you get behind on harvesting, it will produce little white flowers near the tops of the plants. In some vegetables this is a sign to discard the plant, but not with winter purslane. The flowers are edible and look good added to salads.

Sow & Grow

WINTER PURSLANE

(Montia perfoliata)
Purslane family (Portulacaceae)

SOWING
Seed depth: 6mm (¼in)
Germination soil temperature: 10–13°C (50–55°F)
Days to germination: 7–10
Sow indoors: Late autumn to late winter for indoor growing
Sow outdoors: 4 weeks before last frost

GROWING
pH range: 6.5–7.0
Growing soil temperature: 10–18°C (50–65°F)
Spacing in beds: *In rows,* 2.5cm (1in); *in beds,* 20cm (8in); thin to 10–15cm (4–6in)
Watering: Moderate and even; light when grown in a cold frame over winter
Light: Full sun to partial shade
Nutrient requirements: N=low; P=low; K=low
Rotation considerations: Avoid following with radicchio, endive, escarole, artichoke
Good companions: Other salad leaves
Bad companions: None
Seed longevity: 5 years
Seeds per gram: 1,600 (45,000 seeds per oz)

Spinach

In the cartoon universe, Popeye ate a can of spinach and became instantly muscled and strong. In the real world, spinach doesn't work quite that fast, and fresh spinach right from the garden is light-years better than anything in a can. One of the first spring garden greens, spinach is high in vitamins and minerals, has excellent flavour and is easy to grow. And who knows? It might help if you have any problems with the neighbourhood bully.

△ **Muscles in a can?** Along with being highly nutritious, spinach is also versatile in the kitchen. It is delicious raw in salads, and is the basic ingredient in many hot dishes, including lasagne.

SOWING

Spinach germinates and grows best in the cool weather that comes at the beginning and end of the growing season. It's also pretty frost-tolerant. Direct-sow it in the garden in spring as soon as the ground can be worked, or start it in trays indoors three to four weeks before the last frost, for planting out.

Instead of making just one large sowing, you'll get a much bigger crop and much better spinach if you make a series of small successional sowings spaced a week or 10 days apart. Stop sowing the seeds when the warm-weather crops go in, around the last expected frost date, then you can start sowing spinach again when late summer arrives. Its germination is less uniform in warm soil, so you should sow it a bit more thickly in late summer than in spring.

Sow & Grow

SPINACH

(Spinacia oleracea)
Beet family (Chenopodiaceae)

SOWING

Seed depth: 13mm (½in)

Soil temperature: 10–24°C (50–75°F); the optimum is 21°C (70°F)

Days to germination: 7–14

Sow indoors: 3–4 weeks before last frost

Sow outdoors: Early spring

GROWING

pH range: 6.5–7.5

Soil temperature: 16–18°C (60–65°F)

Spacing in beds: 30–45cm (12–18in)

Watering: Light but even

Light: Full sun to partial shade

Nutrient requirements: N=moderate; P=moderate; K=moderate

Rotation considerations: Benefits all crops that it succeeds; should not follow legumes

Good companions: Cabbage family, celery, legumes, lettuce, onion, pea, radish, strawberry

Bad companions: Potato

Seed longevity: 3 years

Seeds per gram: 100 (3,000 seeds per oz)

GROWING

Spinach grows in a wide variety of soils but produces the best crops in those rich in organic matter such as compost. In fertile soil it usually does not require supplementary feeding, and applications of nitrogen should be considered only if the leaves are pale green in colour. Too much nitrogen can give spinach a sharp, metallic flavour.

HARVESTING AND STORING

You can harvest spinach in a variety of ways. Take your pick of any or all:

▶ Begin picking individual leaves as soon as they're big enough to use.

▶ Cut the entire plant at soil level when leaves are large and meaty.

▶ Cut the entire plant 2.5cm (1in) above the soil level. This method encourages the plant to regrow another crop of leaves.

▶ In warm weather, the plants form a central stem that rapidly grows into a flower stalk, a process called bolting. When this occurs, harvest what you can (the flavour of the leaves may be sharper) and put the rest on the compost heap.

A Hot-Weather Look-Alike

If you wish you could have spinach during the hottest days of summer, there is a crop just for you. New Zealand spinach (*Tetragonia expansa*) is actually not a spinach at all but a drought-tolerant maritime succulent. You can grow this vigorous, sprawling plant over a frame, or allow it to spread over the bed.

Because it's frost-sensitive, sow whenever it's safe to plant tomatoes and peppers. Soak seeds overnight before sowing either in stations, like squash, or spaced about 25cm (10in) apart in rows. Harvest the dark green leaves individually as needed.

BEST VARIETIES

Popeye's Choice is slow to bolt and bears large, tender, very flavourful leaves.

Melody is disease resistant and produces large crops of good-flavoured leaves.

Indian Summer is a fast-growing, high-yielding variety with excellent flavour.

Tyee is very slow to bolt. It produces large crops of good-flavoured leaves.

△ **Keep the harvest coming.** You'll often get enough spinach for salads by harvesting just the outer leaves (A) and allowing the rest of the plant to continue to develop. You can also cut the plant about 2.5cm (1in) above the soil (B), and it will grow another batch of leaves.

Squash (Summer)

At first glance, giving advice on how to grow more courgettes seems silly. Who in their right mind wants to grow more courgettes? But there's much, much more to summer squash than just courgettes and marrows. Yellow straightneck squash, crookneck squash, cousa squash, and the delightful pattypan or scallop squash are just a few examples of the other exciting varieties of summer squash.

△ **Squash squad.** Summer squash comes in a surprising variety of shapes and colours, each with subtly different textures and flavours. In almost every case, summer squash is best when picked young and harvested often.

THE SITE

Pretty much the same growing methods work for each of the many types of summer squash. Summer squash is sensitive to cold temperatures and grows best during the long days of summer. If possible, prepare the growing bed in autumn by turning in lots of chopped leaves or compost and covering the bed with leaves and straw.

SOWING

In spring, remove the straw or leaf mulch and warm the soil with black plastic.

Starting seeds indoors. For an early harvest, start plants indoors three or four weeks before the last frost date. Squash does not transplant well, but if you start the plants in 10cm (4in) pots and transplant carefully to avoid

---

Sow & Grow

SUMMER SQUASH

(*Cucurbita pepo*)
Cucumber family
(*Cucurbitaceae*)

SOWING

Seed depth: 1.3–2.5cm (½–1in)

Soil temperature: 21–35°C (70–95°F); the optimum is 35°C (95°F)

Days to germination: 6–10

Sow indoors: 3–4 weeks before last frost

Sow outdoors: When soil temperature reaches 21°C (70°F); use row covers during cold weather

GROWING

pH range: 6.0–6.5

Soil temperature: 18–24°C (65–75°F)

Spacing in beds: 30–45cm (12–18in)

Watering: Heavy and even

Light: Full sun

Nutrient requirements: N=high; P=moderate; K=moderate

Rotation considerations: Avoid following winter squash, pumpkin, cucumber, melon

Good companions: Celeriac, celery, nasturtium, onion, radish, sweetcorn

Bad companions: Potato

Seed longevity: 4 years

Seeds per gram: 10 (300 seeds per oz)

disturbing the roots, they'll be okay. Sow three seeds to a pot and thin to one plant by clipping the extras with scissors. Keep temperatures at about 21°C (70°F). Harden the plants by cutting back on water and gradually lowering the night temperature to about 18°C (65°F) during the week before transplanting.

Direct-sowing. Wait until the soil is 21°C (70°F) or warmer, and then sow three seeds to a station. Space the stations about 45cm (18in) apart. After seedlings have one true leaf, thin to one plant by cutting the others with scissors.

GROWING
After transplanting indoor-started plants, or when direct-sown seedlings emerge, cover the plants with floating plastic mulch if night temperatures dip below 18°C (65°F). This also keeps insect pests at bay while the plants are young and vulnerable.

Ta-Daa!
Most summer squash varieties grow in bush form, but *Tromboncini Alberga*, an heirloom courgette variety from Italy, is a vine – a whole lot of vine. Grow *Tromboncini* on a frame, and pick the curvy fruits when they are 30–37.5cm (12–15in) long. They're firm and tasty, with few seeds. Unlike bush-type courgettes, this plant will produce prolifically for the whole season.

Italian trombone squash, *Tromboncini Alberga*

Squash is a heavy feeder but, when grown in soils rich in organic matter, it rarely needs supplementary feeding. If leaves are pale or plants lack vigour, fertilize with a low-nitrogen fertilizer such as seaweed. Too much fertilizer, especially nitrogen, can limit yields.

HARVESTING AND STORING
The secret to fine squash is more in the harvesting than in the growing. You must pick young, pick small and pick often. Here are some tips on picking the tastiest squash yet.

Courgettes live life in the fast lane. They grow so quickly, it seems as if you could sit in the garden and watch them grow. Once fruits begin to appear, visit your courgettes every day or so. Pick the fruits when they are about 10–12.5cm (4–5in) long. Courgette plants bear for a long time if harvested often but, even with the best of picking, quality and yields start to decline after a month or so. If you're a real courgette fan, plan on a couple of successional sowings about a month apart.

Yellow summer squash includes both straightneck and crookneck types, and each type should be harvested a little differently. Straightneck squash should be picked at about 10–12.5cm (4–5in). At this stage they can be sliced and eaten skin and all. Crookneck squash tends to have a thicker skin earlier than straightneck, so harvest when slightly smaller.

Cousa squash looks like a compromise between a courgette and a straightneck squash, with pale greenish yellow skin and the classic summer squash shape. Although it has a distinctive flavour, it resembles courgettes. Harvest it when it's about 7.5cm (3in) long. The prolific plants will reward frequent harvesting with more fruits.

Scallop or pattypan squash's shape and flavour are unforgettable. The plants bear round, green

△ Costata Romanesca

Sunburst ▷

△ Seneca Prolific

or yellow fruit with scalloped edges. Pick these when they are small, no larger than 10cm (4in) in diameter. They are at their best when they measure from 5–7.5cm (2–3in) across. Harvest often, for when these plants begin bearing they can continue all summer long.

All summer squash keeps in the refrigerator for about two weeks and freezes well.

BEST VARIETIES OF COURGETTE

Costata Romanesca. The perfect ingredient in Mediterranean recipes, this courgette has a clear, distinct flavour. The fruits are pale green and marked with lighter-coloured ribs. Harvest when 15–25cm (6–10in) long. This variety produces a large number of male flowers, which can be picked, dipped in tempura batter and lightly fried. They look and taste spectacular!

Gold Rush looks like a summer squash, with clear, bright yellow skin. Its flavour is very similar to other good courgette varieties, but it is more attractive than most.

Spacemaster. A small courgette, Spacemaster produces lots of fruits on plants a little smaller than standard varieties. It's nicely prolific, so be sure to pick often.

Eight Ball. With dark green, nearly ball-shaped fruits, these plants begin bearing earlier than most varieties, and the little fruits are very tasty indeed.

BEST VARIETIES OF STRAIGHTNECK

Zephyr. An eyecatching squash with a pale yellow top and light green bottom, Zephyr has firm but tender fruits with excellent flavour.

Saffron. This looks and tastes just like a straightneck summer squash should, with rich flavour and clear yellow colour. The plants are nicely compact and produce a lot of fruits.

BEST VARIETIES OF CROOKNECK

Horn of Plenty. Attractive, delicious fruits grow on well-behaved, compact plants, 90cm (3ft) in diameter. Pick the fruits when small and plants will continue to produce for months.

BEST VARIETIES OF PATTYPAN

Sunburst. This prolific and reliable variety produces attractive yellow fruits with a creamy, tasty flesh that can be diced and tossed into mixed vegetable dishes or sautéed all by itself.

Starship. It's good to find a squash with a compact habit. The green, scallop-shaped fruits look like little spaceships. Pick when small for a taste that is out of this world.

Squash (Winter) & Pumpkin

Two things can make me feel rich as winter approaches: a big pile of dry firewood and a wheelbarrow heaped with winter squash. With all the harvesting of tomatoes, peppers and other summer things, for most of the growing season winter squash doesn't get much attention. Yet when the first chilly mornings come, I find myself down in the squash patch thinking of wood smoke, pumpkins and buttery baked squash. Months later, when much of the garden harvest has been eaten, there is still plenty of winter squash in storage.

△ **Winter wonders.** Squash is good for you, because it contains lots of fibre, vitamin A and beta-carotene. All that and it's delicious, too. Acorn, buttercup, butternut, delicata, hubbard, spaghetti squash and pumpkin all fit into the winter squash category.

The Site

Summer squash and winter squash need the same things to grow well – winter squash just needs more of them. Winter squash plants are bigger than their summer counterparts, and those plants produce bigger fruits.

Winter squash needs at least three months of frost-free growing time, and it's particularly

Sow & Grow

Winter Squash & Pumpkin

(Cucurbita spp.) Cucumber family (Cucurbitaceae)

Sowing

Seed depth: 1.3–2.5cm (½–1in)

Soil temperature: 21–32°C (70–90°F); the optimum is 32°C (90°F)

Days to germination: 6–10

Sow indoors: 3–4 weeks before last frost

Sow outdoors: When soil temperature reaches 21°C (70°F); use polytunnels during colder weather

Growing

pH range: 5.5–6.5

Soil temperature: 18–24°C (65–75°F)

Spacing in beds: 30–45cm (12–18in)

Watering: Heavy and even

Light: Full sun

Nutrient requirements: N=high; P=moderate; K=moderate

Rotation considerations: Avoid following summer squash, cucumber, melon

Good companions: Celeriac, celery, onion, radish, sweetcorn

Bad companions: Potato

Seed longevity: 4 years

Seeds per gram: 10 (300 seeds per oz)

frost-sensitive at each end of the growing cycle. Like summer squash, it does not germinate well in cold soil.

Before sowing or transplanting, loosen the soil in an area at least as large as a dustbin lid and 30cm (1ft) or so deep and work in lots of compost or well-rotted manure and some seaweed. Cover an area 90cm (3ft) square with black plastic at least a week before planting. I leave the plastic in place all summer to help with weed control.

SOWING

In warm areas, direct-sow once the soil has warmed in spring and the danger of frost is past. In most areas, however, it's best to start plants indoors three weeks before the last frost date. Avoid starting plants earlier than this, as older plants often do not transplant well. Sow three seeds to a 10cm (4in) pot and thin to one strong plant. Maintain a temperature of about 21°C (70°F) for germination and growth. Transplant carefully, being sure not to disturb the roots.

GROWING

Use protection to maintain proper growth temperatures and protect against insect pests when the plants are small, but remove the covers when flowers appear.

HARVESTING AND STORING

In theory, two characteristics signal that winter squashes are ripe:
▶ The stems begin to shrivel and dry.
▶ The skin is too hard to pierce with your thumbnail (pumpkin skin, however, remains a little soft even when ripe).

In practice, harvest before frost can damage the fruits and so shorten their storage life.

Leave at least 2.5cm (1in) of vine on the fruits. And remember that the stems aren't handles: they can't support the weight of the fruit, and stemless squash or pumpkins don't store well. Winter squash keeps best if it's cured in the sun

The Garden Gorilla

Growing successful winter squash at the same time as growing all your other vegetables depends on what I call the Gorilla Corollary:

Q: 'Where does a gorilla sit?'
A: 'Anywhere it wants to.'

Winter squash are garden gorillas. The vines are so vigorous they will take over vast amounts of the garden if you don't plan ahead. You can exert some control over them by sowing the seed along the edge of your plot. As the vines grow, direct them outward, away from the rest of the vegetable garden. They will run over something, but at least it won't be the rest of your vegetables.

△ **Squash likes it hot.** Winter squash will perform better if you warm the soil with black plastic before planting and then leave the plastic in place, not only to maintain soil temperature, but also to help to control weeds. Cut a circle out of the black plastic, dig a hole deep enough for the plant to be at the height it grew in the pot, and set the plant in place, being especially careful not to damage the plant roots. Finally, firm the soil gently around the transplant.

for a week or so before being placed in storage. Bring it under cover if frost threatens.

Store at 10°C (50°F) where it is moderately dry. Eat acorn, delicata and spaghetti squash first. The flavour of both butternut and buttercup squash is improved by storing them for a few weeks.

BEST ACORN VARIETIES

Acorn squash are small, dark green or mottled, and vaguely acorn shaped. Like many winter squash, they're good baked.

Heart of Gold. A squash with dark green skin with white variegation. The fruits are about 12.5cm (5in) long with firm, well-flavoured, pale orange flesh. The plants are high-yielding but compact.

Tuffy. With very dark green (nearly black), thick rinds protecting succulent yellow flesh, these plants are vigorous and productive.

Table Top. A good squash to use soon after harvest, Table Top produces small, space-saving plants that bear medium to small, golden orange, nicely flavoured squash.

BEST BUTTERCUP VARIETIES

A buttercup squash looks like an acorn squash that somebody sat on. The dark, blackish green rind protects the sweet, yellowish orange flesh. The fruits, while looking a bit compressed, store very well and grow abundantly on vigorous vines.

Burgess. A popular squash with dark green skin and sweet, rich-flavoured flesh, Burgess is productive and vigorous.

Sweet Mama. A hybrid with pleasant-tasting, sweet orange flesh and black-green rind. It's high yielding and the fruits store well.

Autumn Cup. This full-flavoured, sweet-fleshed squash bears medium to small dark green fruits.

△ Heart of Gold

BEST BUTTERNUT VARIETIES

Early Butternut. Medium-sized, light tan fruits that mature early. The orange flesh is smooth and sweet.

Long Island Cheese. This looks more like a small tan pumpkin than a butternut, with deep orange flesh, excellent for pies.

Waltham. A popular butternut, with reliable yields of large, tan fruits with bright orange, smooth, sweet flesh. It stores well and the flavour improves in storage.

BEST HUBBARD SQUASH VARIETIES

Blue Hubbard. These large aqua-blue fruits have sweet, yellow flesh.

Blue Ballet. A smaller version of Blue Hubbard, this squash has cloudy blue skin and sweet orange flesh.

Warted Green Hubbard. A good keeper and large, with green skin and tasty yellow flesh.

BEST PUMPKIN VARIETIES

Atlantic Giant. This is a huge plant, not for the small garden. A single fruit may weigh hundreds of kilos – the heaviest ever grown weighed over 450kg (1,000lb). That's a lot of pumpkin!

The Great Pumpkin. Another large one. Pinkish-orange fruits often weigh over 45kg (100lb).

Howden. Produces well-shaped, 5–9kg (10–20lb) fruits, the perfect size for Halloween.

Wee-B-Little. This miniature has the classic round pumpkin shape. The small 7.5–10cm (3–4in) diameter fruits are perfect for using as table decorations.

OTHER WINTER SQUASH VARIETIES

Lakota. A new variety, Lakota bears teardrop-shaped fruit marked with orange and dark green, with flesh similar to Hubbard types.

Spaghetti. A medium-sized squash with tan skin and yellowish flesh, spaghetti squash is often called vegetable spaghetti. But the flavour is better than any pasta, with a sweet, nutty taste.

Strawberries, Alpine

Many gardeners have a love-hate relationship with strawberries. They love the sweet, juicy fruits but hate the weeds and tangles of runners that overrun garden paths and planting areas. The solution to this dilemma comes in the form of a delicious, well-behaved plant called Alpine strawberry, or fraise du bois.

HARVESTING AND STORING

Harvest Alpine strawberries when the fruits turn crimson. Although they're much smaller than commercial types, these fruits have a rich, tart strawberry flavour, and they bear from spring to autumn. How long they will store is a mystery, as they're always eaten the same day they are picked.

BEST VARIETIES

Among the many fine varieties of Alpine strawberries are Alexandria, Charles V and Pineapple Crush.

Saving Strawberry Seed

Alpine strawberries do not produce runners, but plants can easily be propagated from seed. Collect a handful of ripe strawberries and spread them on newspaper in a warm, dry, sunny room. When dry, work the pieces between your fingers, so the seeds to fall on the newspaper. Dry the seeds for another day or two, and then sow in a tray of seed compost. When the seedlings are about 13mm (½in) tall, transplant them to individual pots. After they've formed a rosette of leaves, plant them in the garden between spring and early autumn.

◁ **Three seasons of strawberries.** Most Alpine strawberries can be bought as plants. You should put them in the ground in spring or autumn. Once they are bearing fruit, harvest them from spring through summer and into autumn.

Sow & Grow

ALPINE STRAWBERRIES

(Fragaria vesca)
Rose family (Rosaceae)

SOWING

Seed depth: 3–6mm (⅛–¼in)

Germination soil temperature: 18–24°C (65–75°F)

Days to germination: 7–14

Sow indoors: 8 weeks before setting out in early spring

Sow outdoors: Not recommended

GROWING

pH range: 5.5–7.0

Growing soil temperature: 16–27°C (60–80°F)

Spacing in beds: 30cm (12in)

Watering: Moderate

Light: Full sun to partial shade

Nutrient requirements: N=moderate; P=moderate; K=moderate

Rotation considerations: Avoid following beetroot, pea, pepper, sweetcorn or tomato

Good companions: Melon

Bad companions: Broccoli and other cabbage family crops

Seed longevity: 1 year

Seeds per gram: 2,450 (70,000 seeds per oz)

Swede

Many people think a swede (rutabaga) is just a big turnip, but turnips and swedes are actually completely different vegetables. The flesh of a turnip is white, while that of a swede is usually yellow. Swedes are more tolerant of cold than turnips, and have a rich, mellow taste that goes well with hearty autumn meals.

◁ **Harvest the heartiness of autumn.** It's usual to dig swedes in mid- to late autumn, after a few frosts but before the ground freezes. The cold weather helps to develop their characteristic flavour.

Strawberries & Swede

SOWING AND GROWING

Work compost or leaf mould into soil before sowing to enrich and loosen it. Sow seeds in early summer or, in cool regions, midsummer.

Swedes need a good supply of potassium and phosphorus, with slightly lower amounts of nitrogen. To meet these needs, fertilize your plants with compost 'tea' throughout the growing season. Boron deficiency can produce a brown staining in the centre of the roots. Protect plants from most insect pests by growing them under floating plastic mulches for the first few weeks.

HARVESTING AND STORING

To harvest, pull or carefully dig the plants and cut the tops 2.5cm (1in) from the top of the root. Store in a cool, damp place with the temperature just above freezing, or place in a plastic vegetable storage bag and keep in the refrigerator. Roots store well for months.

BEST VARIETIES

York. Resistant to clubroot, York stores very well and has a smooth, rich flavour.

Thomson Laurentian. This variety has good flavour and stores well.

Gilfeather. An heirloom variety, Gilfeather has a white root crowned with a cap of purple. The flesh is very sweet and mild, with just a slight hint of pungency.

Joan. This swede has excellent, sweet flavour.

Sow & Grow

SWEDE

(Brassica napus)
Cabbage family (Cruciferae)

SOWING

Seed depth: 13mm (½in)

Soil temperature: 16–29°C (60–85°F); the optimum is 29°C (85°F)

Days to germination: 3–5

Sow indoors: Not recommended

Sow outdoors: Early spring

GROWING

pH range: 6.4–7.2

Soil temperature: 16–18°C (60–65°F)

Spacing in beds: 20cm (8in)

Watering: Moderate

Light: Best in full sun; will tolerate light shade

Nutrient requirements: N=low; P=moderate; K=moderate

Rotation considerations: Good succession crop after spring onion

Good companions: Nasturtium, onion family, pea

Bad companions: Potato

Seed longevity: 4 years

Seeds per gram: 400 (11,000 seeds per oz)

Sweetcorn

A satisfying ear of sweetcorn shouldn't taste like sugar – it should taste like sweetcorn. It seems to me that every year the seed catalogues feature a new variety of sweetcorn supposedly far sweeter than last year's sweetest. Personally, I'm not a fan of supersweet corn. The main virtue of these new varieties is commercial: their sugar is slow to convert to starch after harvest, so they can mimic fresh sweetcorn even after a long trip to the supermarket and a wait on the shelves. That isn't necessary with homegrown sweetcorn.

If you find that there's not enough 'sweet' in your homegrown sweetcorn, the problem is more likely to be the way in which you're growing it rather than the variety you are growing. Providing you give your sweetcorn good growing conditions you will be rewarded with corn that is both sweet and well-flavoured.

△ **Summer rewards.** Sweetcorn likes it sunny and hot, with ample soil moisture and consistent fertility. Given these things, corn will reward you with a crop that sings summer.

Sow & Grow

SWEETCORN

(Zea mays)
Grass family (Poaceae)

SOWING

Seed depth: 2.5cm (1in)
Germination soil temperature: 27°C (80°F)
Days to germination: 4
Sow indoors: Not recommended
Sow outdoors: 1 week after last frost

GROWING

pH range: 6.0–7.0
Growing soil temperature: 18–24°C (65–75°F)

Spacing in beds: 20cm (8in)
Watering: Moderate early; heavy from flowering to harvest
Light: Full sun
Nutrient requirements: N=high; P=high; K=high
Rotation considerations: Precede with a nitrogen-fixing crop
Good companions: Beetroot, cabbage, cantaloupe, cucumber, dwarf bean, marrow, parsley, pea, early potato, pumpkin, winter squash
Bad companions: Tomato
Seed longevity: 1–2 years
Seeds per gram: 5 (150 seeds per oz)

THE SITE

Begin preparing the sweetcorn bed in autumn. Apply at least 2.5cm (1in) of compost or rotted manure and work it into the soil with a garden fork. To encourage worm activity, mulch the bed before a frost.

SOWING

In spring, remove the mulch to let the soil begin heating, and apply some finished compost. Cover the sweetcorn beds with black plastic at least a week before sowing and monitor soil temperature with a soil thermometer.

Sow the seeds 2.5cm (1in) deep and 20cm (8in) apart, down the centre of a 75cm (30in) bed. To ensure good pollination, plant each variety in blocks of four short rows, rather than as a single long row. Sow new blocks every two weeks for successive harvests throughout the season.

After sowing, keep the soil moist and install a floating fleece mulch supported by hoops to maintain soil temperature and protect seedlings against frost. You can remove the cover when night temperatures are consistently above 16°C (60°F).

GROWING

Sweetcorn is a heavy feeder – a really heavy feeder – particularly of nitrogen. Yet for a plant of its large size, it does not have a very deep or extensive root system: a good blast of wind can flatten it. This means that sweetcorn needs deeply cultivated, fertile soil with readily available nutrients. This allows the plant to produce roots that compensate in density for what they lack in range.

Like other plants with relatively shallow roots, sweetcorn is sensitive to fluctuations in soil moisture, which stress the plants. Regular and shallow cultivation controls weeds while making nutrients available. Water regularly and feed every two weeks with a complete organic fertilizer such as fish, blood and bonemeal, or similar liquid formulation.

△ **A moisture lifeline.** Drip irrigation laid between the rows of sweetcorn gets the right amount of moisture right to the roots.

△ **Sunken treasure.** In dry areas, plant sweetcorn in groups of four, slightly below the level of the bed. The 'bowl' that is created will collect every drop of precious water from rain or irrigation.

Keep Those Sweets Apart

If you grow any of the supersweet varieties, they must be isolated from normal sugar-enhanced types to prevent cross-pollination. You can do this either by keeping the plantings at least 7.5m (25ft) apart or by sowing the seeds of one at least 10 days after you sow the seeds of the other, so that they flower at different times.

HARVESTING

It's easy to know when to pick a ripe tomato, but knowing when to harvest sweetcorn is a little trickier. The secret is to examine the silk at the top of the ear. A ripe ear of sweetcorn will have a small amount of pliant, greenish silk near the top of the husk, with dry, brownish silk at the ends.

The best time of day to pick is another question, and it's one about which you'll hear different advice. Very soon after picking, the sugar in sweetcorn begins turning to starch. Some people like to pick their sweetcorn a few minutes before it gets dropped into the cooking pot. These people believe the faster an ear of corn moves from the garden to your plate, the sweeter it will taste. It makes sense. Yet sweetcorn actually has its highest sugar content in the early morning, not just before the evening meal. The old-timers I've known pick their corn early in the morning, before it's warmed by the sun, and refrigerate it in the husk until supper. I've tried both ways and come to the conclusion that the old-timers are right.

△ **You break it, you buy it.** When it's nearly butter-and-corn-on-the-cob time, it's very tempting to open the husks when the ears are still on the stalk. But because the husk protects the corn, you should open it only when the pot is boiling and you're ready to cook. Instead of peeping, feel the husk to see if it seems full and rounded and look for greenish, pliant silk turned drier and brown at the very ends.

BEST VARIETIES OF SWEETCORN

There are many excellent varieties of sweetcorn. The trick to selecting the best ones is to bypass the supersweet hype and focus on flavour, ears per stalk, number of rows per ear and, one more time – flavour. Here are some of the best bets.

Double Gem is an early bicolour variety that combines fine taste with high yield.

Sugar Snow is a variety that yields large ears filled with sweet, snow-white kernels.

Seneca Arrowhead is a disease-tolerant, early variety with excellent flavour.

Sundance is a vigorous variety, resistant to cold soil, with tasty ears.

◁ **Barbecued corn.** Try the fresh cobs cooked on the barbecue (or even under the grill), turning them until evenly toasted golden brown. Strip back the husks and silk before cooking but leave the husks attached to form a handle.

Field Corn

Field corn is grown mainly as animal feed and for grinding into cornmeal and flour. It is a term that lumps dent, flint and flour corn into one category. The names of these types are unimaginative but accurate:

▸ **Dent corn** has a dent in each kernel when dry.

▸ **Flint corn** has rock-hard kernels.

▸ **Flour corn** makes the best-quality corn flour.

To harvest field corn, allow the husks to dry completely. Unlike most other corns, you can harvest field corn after a few frosts. Husk the ears and bring them to a cool, dry, well-ventilated space to finish drying. Store the kernels on the cob or strip them and store in covered glass containers.

Popcorn

Like field corn and ornamental corn (which bears cobs in a range of startling colours), popcorn has a higher starch content than sweetcorn, but the growing requirements for all of these are the same as for sweetcorn. The difference is in the harvesting.

Popcorn has been part of people's diets for millennia and is eaten all around the world. Native Americans grew it for thousands of years before it became an essential part of a trip to the cinema. Yet in many parts of the world, most people's experience of popcorn nowadays is still limited to the snack aisle of the supermarket.

Popcorn comes in many varieties, from red and blue to white and yellow. It takes longer to mature than sweetcorn, so choose a variety that has enough time to develop in a typical growing season in your area.

Best Varieties of Popcorn

Tom Thumb. An heirloom variety that is early-maturing, Tom Thumb has short stalks and bears yellow kernels.

Robust. This is gourmet-quality, tender popcorn with golden-yellow kernels.

Ruby Red. The burgundy-red kernels are as decorative as they are tasty.

Shaman's Blue. This variety has decorative bluish red kernels.

Top Pop. A tall variety producing plentiful yellow kernels.

Popcorn That Really Pops

Successful popcorn growing means growing popcorn that pops. For a kernel to pop, it must have just the right amount of moisture inside it, and this is influenced by curing.

Harvest before a frost, when the husks have dried and the kernels are shiny, plump and well-coloured. Remove the husks and spread the ears out in a cool, well-ventilated space.

After they have cured for about a month, test-pop some kernels. If they pop nicely, remove them from the cobs and store in dark glass containers. If they pop weakly, they still contain too much moisture. Continue curing, but test-pop every few days, because you don't want them to get too dry.

Sweet Potatoes

Few things are as tasty as sweet potato pie – unless, of course, it's sweet potato chips sprinkled with cinnamon and dipped in tangy mustard. Sweet potatoes are the roots of a vine native to tropical America, and the crop is identified with warm regions, but with a little gentle persuasion this hearty vegetable will provide even gardeners in cooler parts with a large, sweet harvest.

PLANTING

Most vegetables are grown from seeds, but sweet potatoes are grown from rooted cuttings. The cuttings, called slips or draws, are produced from the sprouts of sweet potato roots. You can buy slips at garden centres, by mail order and on the Internet. It's also easy to make your own slips, and it's such fun that most people prefer to do it themselves. (See What a Slip! in the box opposite.)

△ **A welcome vine.** Sweet potatoes are ready for harvest from this prolific vine three to four months after planting, as the heart-shaped leaves begin to turn yellow, but they do need to be harvested before the first autumn frost.

Sow & Grow

SWEET POTATOES

(*Ipomoea batatas*)
Morning glory family
(Convolvulaceae)

SOWING

Seed depth: Not applicable

Germination soil temperature: Not applicable

Days to germination: Not applicable

Sow indoors: Not applicable

Transplant outdoors: 2 weeks after last frost

GROWING

pH range: 5.5–6.5

Growing soil temperature: 18–32°C (65–90°F)

Spacing in beds: 35–45cm (14–18in)

Watering: Low

Light: Full sun

Nutrient requirements: N=low; P=low; K=low

Rotation considerations: Avoid following root crops

Good companions: Marigold

Bad companions: Beetroot, carrot, potato

Seed longevity: Not applicable

Seeds per gram: Not applicable

GROWING

When all danger of frost is past, set the slips in the garden in loose, fertile soil that has been improved with compost. Fertilize only if the plants do not appear healthy, as too much nitrogen will diminish yield and produce long, thin roots.

HARVESTING AND STORING

You can harvest sweet potatoes as soon as they reach usable size, which will usually be after a period of about 100 to 140 days from planting, depending on variety. Be sure to harvest them before the first frost; cold weather can damage the roots. If you can't harvest and a frost is coming, mulch the area heavily with straw before sunset.

To harvest, cut back the vines and lift the roots from the ground with a garden fork. Do this gingerly, as the skins of sweet potatoes bruise easily.

Cure the roots before storing by letting them lie out in the sun for a day, and then move them to a shady area that will stay at about 27°C (80°F) for a week to ten days. After this the roots should store well for about six months in a cool, damp place. If your passion for sweet potatoes is such that your harvest will be eaten in only a few months, full curing isn't necessary.

BEST VARIETIES

Beauregard. This sweetheart of a sweet potato has large, dark burgundy-purple roots and pumpkin-orange flesh. Meaty, with a smooth, dessertlike texture, Beauregard matures quickly and is excellent for all your sweet potato recipes.

Vardaman. A nice variety for those who love to eat sweet potatoes but are short of space to grow them. This bush variety takes up less space than most trailing varieties and is capable of out-yielding them, too. The roots are large, with deep orange, finely flavoured flesh.

What a Slip!

To make sweet potato slips, purchase large, firm sweet potatoes about 30 to 40 days before the last frost. You can either set the sweet potatoes in sand in a warm, sunny room or greenhouse, or cut them into sections and place each section in a glass of water with one half immersed and the remaining half above the water. Shoots will then rise from the cut section.

When the shoots are about 10–15cm (4–6in) long, gently twist them from the section of potato. Collect the shoots and put them in a container of water so that only their bottom halves are immersed. Slips are ready to plant when roots appear, usually in just a few days. Don't allow the roots to get longer than 2.5–5cm (1–2in) before planting.

△ **Preparing sweet potato slips.** These shoots are just about ready to be pulled from the section of rooting potato. We'll put them in water, half submerged, and in a few days roots will appear and the slips will be ready for planting.

Swiss Chard

Many years ago, a cartoonist called Al Capp conceived a creature called the Schmoo. Its mission in life was to become whatever you wanted it to be. I used to think the Schmoo was just a fantasy, until I discovered Swiss chard. Swiss chard is the vegetable garden's Schmoo. You want salad? Greens? Some spinach, even though all the spinach bolted a long time ago? Asparagus in late summer? And you want all of this from a single plant that carries on producing until there is a really hard frost, with almost no need for care along the way? And you would like all of these things in bright shiny colours? You've got it, if you planted Swiss chard.

△ **Turn up the lights.** Who says you need to hide vegetables from view? Few ornamental plants can boast the long-season health, vigour and colour of Swiss chard, especially in varieties such as Bright Lights.

SOWING AND GROWING

How close together you grow Swiss chard plants depends on how you want to harvest them. If you plan to cut the whole plant, space them about 10–12.5cm (4–5in) apart. If you plan to harvest the outer stalks continuously throughout the season, space plants about 20–25cm (8–10in) apart to accommodate their greater size.

Sow & Grow

SWISS CHARD

(Beta vulgaris) Cicla group
Beet family (Chenopodiaceae)

SOWING

Seed depth: 13mm (½in)

Soil temperature: 10–29°C (50–85°F); the optimum is 29°C (85°F)

Days to germination: 5–7

Sow indoors: 1–2 weeks before last frost

Sow outdoors: After last frost

GROWING

pH range: 6.0–7.0

Soil temperature: Above 10°C (50°F); the optimum is 16–18°C (60–65°F)

Spacing in beds: *For harvesting entire plant,* 10–12.5cm (4–5in) apart in a staggered pattern; *for harvesting outer leaves,* 20–25cm (8–10in) apart in a staggered pattern

Watering: Moderate and even

Light: Best in full sun, tolerates light shade

Nutrient requirements: N=low; P=moderate; K=moderate

Rotation considerations: Avoid following beetroot, spinach, orache; benefits following a legume crop

Good companions: Cabbage family, legumes, lettuce

Bad companions: Beetroot, orache, spinach

Seed longevity: 4 years

Seeds per gram: 50 (1,500 seeds per oz)

If you plan to remove whole plants, be sure to sow successively throughout summer and early autumn. Swiss chard can endure light frosts in spring and moderate frosts in autumn.

Whatever spacing you choose, maintain a thin layer of compost on the bed to ensure sufficient nutrients for the plants. But this is a crop that is forgiving of neglect.

HARVESTING AND STORING

You can begin harvesting the leaves when plants are about 15–20cm (6–8in) tall. You have a choice of harvesting methods:

▶ Harvest the whole plant; the leaves and stems are especially tender.

▶ Cut the young plants 2.5cm (1in) above the soil; they will continue to grow so that you can harvest them again and again.

▶ Cut leaves from the outside of the plant, leaving the heart, which will continue to grow.

BEST VARIETIES

Charlotte. A truly stunning variety that is as attractive to look at as it is delicious to eat. Charlotte has large, cherry-red stalks and crinkled, dark green leaves.

Cutups. (A) If you cut only the outer stalks, a few Swiss chard plants will offer you a continuous supply of food over several months. (B) You can also cut the entire plant about 2.5cm (1in) above the soil; another plant will grow from the crown to provide you with a second harvest.

△ Swiss chard Charlotte

Bright Lights. Like a display of northern lights in the garden, Bright Lights is a rainbow disguised as a vegetable. The delicious stalks (which taste a bit like asparagus when steamed) come in five colours – white, red, yellow, pink and orange. The colours fade when the stalks are cooked, but the flavour does not.

Bright Yellow. The brightest light of Bright Lights has a show of its own. Bright Yellow has lemon-yellow stems beneath deeply crinkled, dark green leaves. And, of course, it is delicious.

Fordhook Giant. There are many new and colourful varieties of Swiss chard, but this long-time favourite is the standard they must measure up to. Fordhook Giant is sure to satisfy with its large, meaty stems and thick, tasty leaves.

Argentata. An excellent and popular variety of Swiss chard, with crisp leaves and strong, well-flavoured stems.

Tomatillos

What I like about meeting new people is that I might be meeting a new friend. So it was with my introduction to tomatillos. My first thought was, What a strange-looking vegetable! – all green and wrapped up in a husk that looks like a small brown paper bag. But this plant's in a league by itself. Tomatillos are an affordable luxury in the garden, and their plump, firm fruits are the key ingredient in salsa verde, as well as many other Mexican dishes. The plants are easy to grow and hardier than tomatoes, while also less likely to be bothered by pests and diseases. I like making new friends.

SOWING AND GROWING

You grow tomatillos in much the same way you grow tomatoes. Start the seed off indoors in late winter or early spring, and then move the transplants to the garden after the last frost. Set the plants deep in the soil, with only the top few leaves poking above ground. Tomatillos are rangy plants that can spread more than 1.2m (4ft), so give them plenty of room. You can support them on a frame, but they seem to grow best if allowed to run free. Fertilizing isn't needed.

HARVESTING AND STORING

Harvesting usually begins about two months after transplanting. When a tomatillo is ripe, its husk usually splits. It may also be ripe when the fruit begins to soften and fills out the husk well.

BEST VARIETIES

Purple. Aptly named, this tomatillo has deep purple skin.

De Milpa. A nearly self-reliant heirloom, De Milpa stores well.

Toma Verde. This variety is early and reliable.

◁ **Good taste:** Tomatillos have been a favourite of many people for generations. If you haven't tried them yet, I'm sure you'll to be pleasantly surprised.

Sow & Grow

TOMATILLOS
(Physalis ixocarpa)
Tomato family (Solanaceae)

SOWING

Seed depth: 6mm (¼in)

Germination soil temperature: 21–27°C (70–80°F)

Days to germination: 7–14

Sow indoors: 4 weeks before last frost

GROWING

pH range: 6.0–7.0

Growing soil temperature: 16–27°C (60–80°F)

Spacing in beds: 75cm (30in)

Watering: Moderate

Light: Full sun

Nutrient requirements: N=low; P=low; K=low

Rotation considerations: Avoid following aubergine, potato, pepper, tomato; avoid following legumes because there may be too much nitrogen in the soil

Good companions: Asparagus, basil, dwarf bean, cabbage family, carrot, celery, chive, cucumber, garlic, lettuce, marigold, mint, nasturtium, onion, parsley, pepper, pot marigold

Bad companions: Climbing bean, dill, fennel, potato

Seed longevity: 3 years

Seeds per gram: 600 (17,000 seeds per oz)

T

Tomatoes

If there's something more delectable than a fresh tomato sandwich for lunch in late summer, I haven't experienced it. And tomato sandwiches are just the beginning. There's also pasta sauce made from meaty plum tomatoes, flavourful cherry tomatoes tossed in salads, and fried green tomatoes and tomato pickles made from fruits gathered at the end of the season. Tomatoes have something for everyone, which is why they have been the most popular vegetable among gardeners for many years.

△ **Queen of the garden.** If gardeners grow only one vegetable, it's often tomatoes. There's no secret to why this is so: you just haven't tasted a tomato until you've picked a ripe one from the vine and eaten it while it's still warm from the sun.

THE SITE

Tomatoes prefer a light, fertile soil with plenty of organic matter. Soils with high levels of nutrients, especially nitrogen, reduce yields. Turn some chopped leaves into the soil in autumn, or add compost in spring. A few weeks before transplanting, cover the growing beds with black plastic to warm the soil.

SOWING

If you have a sunny window, or better still growing lights, and a bit of patience, you're most likely to end up with the biggest, best and tastiest tomatoes if you raise your own seedlings. You'll have to take a few extra steps, but the technique isn't difficult.

Sow & Grow

TOMATOES

(Lycopersicon lycopersicum)
Tomato family (Solanaceae)

SOWING

Seed depth: 13mm (½in)

Soil temperature: 27°C (80°F)

Days to germination: 6–8

Sow indoors: 6–7 weeks before last frost

Plant outdoors: After all danger of frost is past

GROWING

pH range: 5.8–7.0

Soil temperature: 21°C (70°F)

Spacing in beds: *Supported,* 37.5cm (15in); *unsupported determinates,* 60cm (2ft); *unsupported indeterminates,* 90cm (3ft)

Watering: Moderate to high during growth, low during harvest

Light: Full sun

Nutrient requirements: N=high; P=high; K=high

Rotation considerations: Avoid following potato, pepper, aubergine

Good companions: Asparagus, basil, cabbage family, carrot, celery, chive, cucumber, dwarf bean, garlic, head lettuce, marigold, mint, nasturtium, onion, parsley, pepper, pot marigold

Bad companions: Dill, fennel, potato, climbing bean

Seed longevity: 4 years

Seeds per gram: 1,200 (34,000 per oz)

Germinating seeds. Tomato seedlings are especially susceptible to damping-off disease, so be sure to use a soilless seed compost for your seed trays. Six or seven weeks before the expected planting date, sow seeds 13mm (½in) deep and 2.5cm (1in) or so apart in trays, or two or three to a cell in growing cells. Keep the containers warm at 21–32°C (70–90°F); the optimum is 29°C (85°F). Above the refrigerator may give just the right amount of heat. Germination is much slower at lower temperatures. Keep the soil moist but not wet.

Caring for young seedlings. Once the seeds have germinated, move them to a sunny windowsill or put them under growing lights. If you use growing lights instead of natural light, position the bulbs 2.5–5cm (1–2in) above the plants to stop them becoming thin and leggy.

A purple colour in the leaves is a sign of phosphorus deficiency; use a high-phosphorus liquid fertilizer, if necessary. Otherwise, feed once with a balanced formulation.

Transplanting seedlings. Ten days after germination, transplant to 5cm (2in) pots. Clip away all the leaves except those within the top 2.5cm (1in), and then replant the seedling. Additional roots will grow from the buried stem section, strengthening the plant. Feed with an organic liquid fertilizer – a seaweed formulation is good – and grow in full sun at 16–21°C (60–70°F).

Two weeks after this transplanting, replant again, this time into 10cm (4in) pots. Bury all but the top 5cm (2in) of the plant, removing any leaves that would be below soil level, as before. Water regularly but lightly, just enough to keep the growing medium from drying out.

△ **Nursery tales.** Your local greenhouse or garden centre often carries a wide choice of varieties that will do well in your area. Be sure to visit early in the season for the best selection.

Hardening off. At least two weeks before the plants go into the garden, begin to harden them by moving them outdoors to a sheltered place, increasing their time outdoors a little every day. If you've been growing them in a cold frame, simply lift the top of the frame, each day increasing the time it's open.

BUYING TOMATO PLANTS

A good tomato crop begins with vigorous, compact seedlings about six to seven weeks old in 10cm (4in) pots. Many gardeners like to start their own plants, not only because they can lower the cost and ensure the quality of their crop, but also because many tomato varieties, including some of the best-tasting ones, are not commercially available as plants. But this situation is changing as more nurseries offer heirloom varieties, so it's worth checking around to see what's available near you. And take note of the following.

Buy early. You'll have the best selection at the garden centre if you get there early, and you'll have more control over how the plants are fed, watered and hardened off during their early development. Most of the problems that can lower yield and decrease fruit size happen right at the beginning.

Buy young. The larger and older a plant is when it goes into the ground, the more likely it is to be stressed and set back. Tomatoes should be planted in the garden at roughly the last frost date and should be no more than six to eight weeks old at that time. Try to find out when the seeds were sown. Many nurseries start plants too early. Above all, avoid tall, leggy plants or those with open flowers or fruit.

Buy 10cm (4in) pots. Seedlings grown in anything smaller than a 10cm (4in) pot are likely to be potbound, and a potbound plant is already severely stressed. At this stage in the plant's development, a good root system is much more important than luxuriant top growth. This is why 'bargain' plants grown in small cells or six to a tray are not bargains at all. Turn the pot over and check to be sure no roots are beginning to creep out of the drainage hole. If the nursery owner allows it, gently remove the plant from the pot to see that roots have not started to develop around the sides of the rootball.

PLANTING

The usual advice about when to put tomato seedlings in the garden is 'after the last frost date' but that is a little vague, especially because the crucial variables that

Daily Brushing

Brush the tops of young plants lightly with your hand twice a day. The back-and-forth movement of the stem stimulates the production of hormones called cytokinins, which promote thicker, stronger stems. Outdoors, gentle breezes make this happen naturally.

you need to keep in mind are soil temperature and night-time air temperature. The soil temperature should be at least 13–16°C (55–60°F), and night-time air temperatures should not go below 7°C (45°F) unless you are using row covers to protect the plants. You can guess, or alternatively you can measure the critical temperatures with soil and air thermometers.

Set supported plants 37.5 cm (15in) apart in a single row down the middle of a 75cm (30in) bed. If you aren't using any kind of support, allow 60cm (2ft) for determinate varieties and 90cm (3ft) for indeterminate. Determinate varieties are sensitive to transplant shock, so be very careful not to disturb their roots.

Tomatoes are native to South America, where they get longer and warmer growing seasons than in most parts of northern Europe. Growing good tomato crops consistently involves setting out well-started plants and then using some tricks to convince them that the growing season is longer and warmer than it really is.

Planting Tomatoes in the Garden

1 Dig a hole at least 15cm (6in) in diameter and deep enough so that only about 10cm (4in) of the plant will be above the soil. Use scissors to clip off any leaves that will be buried.

2 Set the plant in the prepared hole. Fill with soil and firm the soil gently around the plant. Water well. This planting method encourages a deep root system, which especially benefits tomatoes during prolonged drought and/or hot weather.

Alternative Tomato-Planting Method

This planting method encourages a shallow root system, which can work well in cool regions, but the technique also leaves plants more susceptible to drought and root damage from cultivation.

Dig a trench 5–7.5cm (2–3in) deep and long enough for all but about 10cm (4in) of the plant. Lay the plant in the trench, gently turning the top upward and packing soil against the stem to support it. Cover with soil and water well.

GROWING

Fertilizing. Water newly planted tomato plants with a dilute solution of compost 'tea', a seaweed-based formulation, or another form of natural fertilizer. Tomatoes can grow quite large so they will need plenty of nutrients to support them; plan on supplementary feeding every two or three weeks.

Protection. Row covers help maintain warmth and deter insects; remove them when flowers appear or when daytime temperatures reach 29°C (85°F).

Mulching. Studies have shown that tomatoes produce earlier and set more fruit when they are mulched with red plastic, which both warms the soil and reflects certain wavelengths of sunlight. Red plastic does not suppress weeds as well as black plastic, though. I have also found that plants do not get enough water through the planting holes in plastic. I deal with both problems successfully by making the plastic removable, and checking weed growth and soil moisture periodically.

If you don't use plastic mulch, you may want to mulch with grass clippings or straw to keep the soil moist. Make sure the soil is well warmed up before you apply the mulch. In cold areas, most gardeners don't use any organic mulch and even avoid companion planting,

◁ **Seeing red.** Red plastic mulch has characteristics that lead to earlier and larger tomato harvests. Lay the plastic on the bed in the same way you put down other plastic mulches and cut a circle into the plastic where you want to place each plant.

so that nothing interferes with maximum soil warming. In warm climates, however, it can get too hot even for tomatoes. In these conditions, organic mulch, or 'living mulch' companion plantings, can be a big help.

Pruning. This is optional for determinate tomatoes. However, pruning is highly recommended for indeterminate varieties, particularly if you grow them on a frame or stake. Don't do any pruning until the plant has been growing in the garden for a week or so. From then on, remove all suckers – the non-flowering stems that grow between the main stem and the leaf axils. Pruning directs the growth to a single main stem. Repeat the process once a week.

◁ **Don't be a sucker.** Pinch or cut out all of the non-flowering stems that grow between the main stem and the leaf axils (A). These stems are aptly called 'suckers', because they take up nutrients that are better used by developing fruits. When the plant reaches the top of the support, prune the tip to stop further top growth (B).

Training. There are many ways to train tomatoes, and all work reasonably well. You can use 'cages' for supports, or you can train the vines to a stake by tying the main stem loosely to the support with twist-ties, twine or torn strips of fabric. Some people think old nylon stockings are best. Be sure to put the stake in the ground at the same time that you plant the tomatoes, to avoid damage to a developing root system.

My favourite method is to train tomatoes around taut twine suspended from a frame. Whichever method you choose, be sure to train or tie the plants to the support weekly, at the same time that you prune them.

HARVESTING

As the autumn frost date approaches, remove the bottom leaves, flowers, and any fruits that will not ripen before the end of the growing season: the hard-as-rock, small green ones.

△ **A lot at stake.** Staking is one traditional method for keeping indeterminate tomatoes under control. Continue to tie up the main stem once a week, when you prune. This should be enough to ensure a well-maintained crop of tomatoes.

△ **Doing the twist.** My favourite method for growing tomatoes is to train them around twine suspended from a frame and then to securely stake them into the soil beneath. Like other methods for growing tomatoes, once-a-week attention is all that's required. Just gently flip the growing end of the plant round the twine. If you like, you can allow a second stem to develop near the base of the plant, simply add another length of twine a few centimetres away from the first one, to help support the second stem as it grows.

A Determined Plant

The various kinds of tomatoes differ in size, colour, disease resistance and the time they take to ripen, but the most important difference for the gardener is growth habit: some tomatoes are determinate, some indeterminate.

Determinate plants, better described as bushes than vines, reach a certain size, flower, set fruit, and then more or less stop growing. You can grow determinate tomatoes without any support at all, allowing them to sprawl along the ground, but they'll do better if you surround them with a low cage-type support. Either way, they don't have to be pruned.

Indeterminate plants are true vines. They grow and set fruit continuously, resulting in much larger plants with a higher foliage-to-fruit ratio. And the bigger the plant, the better the fruit. This means that most of the tomato varieties reputed to have the best flavour are indeterminates. Although they take more work to grow, because they need to be grown on a frame and kept pruned, for tomato lovers the reward is worth the investment. Not only is the flavour of indeterminates better, but you'll get more and bigger fruits, you'll get them sooner, and you'll lose fewer fruits to rot, insects and slugs. You'll also get a much higher yield per square metre of garden by training and pruning: untrained tomatoes take up a great deal of space.

Removing this material directs all the plant's energy toward ripening the rest of the fruits.

The best tomatoes are vine-ripened, but be careful not to leave them on the vine too long. Pick the fruit when the skin of the tomato yields slightly to finger pressure. The shoulder of the fruit is the last part to change colour. Some varieties can be completely ripe and still have yellowish shoulders. You can extend the ripening season through light frosts by draping the frame with a sheet of clear plastic and closing the ends with clothes pegs.

Before a hard frost, pick any tomatoes that show a light yellowing at the shoulders. Most of them will ripen indoors perfectly well. Don't just throw out the green ones though; you can make delicious green-tomato pickles with them.

BEST VARIETIES OF TOMATOES FOR WARM REGIONS

Floramerica. An award-winning tomato, Floramerica bears large, evenly red fruit and is disease resistant to boot.

Solar Set. This variety produces large crops of big red tomatoes in temperatures where other varieties wilt.

Duke. The large red fruit and reliable crops of Duke have made this disease-resistant variety a favourite in warm-region gardens for years.

△ **Diversity in tomatoes.** If you have room, try growing many different kinds of tomatoes. One year certain varieties do better; another year you'll find a different batch more successful. From left to right, in this group are (top row) Amish Paste, Rose and Brandywine; (second row) Roma, Rutgers, Orange Dust and Moskvich; (bottom row) three Sungolds and Glacier.

Best Varieties of Tomatoes for Cool Regions

Moskvich. Originally from Siberia, this variety of tomato produces round, medium-sized, red fruits that have a delicious full flavour.

Oregon Spring. Gardeners that have short growing seasons will be able to enjoy bountiful crops of large, tasty fruits about two months after transplanting Oregon Spring.

△ Moskvich

Best Varieties of Heritage Tomatoes

Rose. This heritage variety might steal your heart. The plants bear large, deep rose red fruits with high shoulders, good shape and flavour as good as any tomato out there, bar none.

German. These very large, beefsteak-type tomatoes have a full, rich flavour. Their fruits are medium red, with irregular yellow ribs on the shoulders.

Brandywine. This large, ribbed fruit is noted for its rich, aromatic flavour. A yellow form, aptly called Yellow Brandywine, produces large, though sometimes irregularly shaped, fruit, which have a slightly softer flavour than Brandywine's.

△ Rose

△ Shumway German

Best Varieties of Small-Fruited Tomatoes

Sweet 100 Plus. Easy to grow, Sweet 100 Plus bears more crack-resistant fruit than regular Sweet 100 and produces abundant clusters of small, cherry-sized tomatoes with a fine sweet taste.

Sun Gold. These small, juicy fruits with a golden-yellow skin are mild-flavoured and a nice addition to summer salads.

Matt's Wild Cherry. With a flavour that rivals larger main-crop varieties, Matt's Wild Cherry bears buckets of very small, ruby-red fruit.

△ Sun Gold

Best Plum Tomatoes

Juliet. A tomato that is at home anywhere, from salad bowl to fresh salsa to pasta sauce.

Tuscany. These medium-sized, firm red fruits are excellent dried or used in cooking.

Milano. An old Italian hybrid, Milano is disease-resistant, with high yields of deep red fruit.

Amish Paste. This heritage variety is versatile. Its fruits can be used for sauces, sliced, or eaten fresh.

San Remo. A very large plum tomato with Jack-in-the-beanstalk vigour. The fruit is tangy-sweet with few seeds, making it perfect for drying or cooking.

Best Main Season Tomatoes

Big Beef. An award-winning, large tomato, Big Beef just bursts with juicy tomato flavour. Disease-resistant plants produce heavy yields earlier in the season than other large-fruited tomato varieties.

Celebrity. An old favourite, Celebrity has medium-sized, deep red fruit, well-shaped and tasty. It's disease resistant, vigorous and very reliable.

Turnips

Turnips are one of those vegetables with a split personality. In some regions turnips are grown as greens, and in other areas they are grown for their roots. The truth is that turnip leaves and turnip roots are both delicious, and each year I look forward to enjoying both.

◁ **Look what turned up!** Turnips taste best when you harvest them in cool weather. Plant a crop in midsummer and enjoy these sweet root vegetables all autumn.

SOWING AND GROWING

Turnips like cool weather, so they're an excellent spring crop – especially when sown with peas. Some people think that the peas actually help the turnips grow.

Fertilizing. Turnips' large root systems need deep, loose soil with lots of organic matter to grow their best. Given these conditions, they don't usually need supplementary feeding.

Watering. Turnips need only a moderate amount of water. To prevent foliar diseases, be sure to avoid wetting the tops.

HARVESTING AND STORING

Leaves. Begin harvesting turnip leaves when the plants are young (but don't take too many, or root growth will slow down). You can either cook the roots with the leaves or use the leaves raw in salads.

Roots. Harvest the roots when they are between 2.5cm (1in) and 7.5cm (3in) in diameter. Larger turnips develop a strong, unappealing flavour. Although you can store roots in the refrigerator for a short time, they are best eaten fresh.

BEST VARIETIES

De Milan. Tender De Milan matures early, and is easy to grow.

Purple Top White Globe. The most popular garden turnip for many years, Purple Top White Globe produces fine-flavoured roots and tender leaves.

Sow & Grow

TURNIPS

(Brassica rapa)
Cabbage family (Cruciferae)

SOWING

Seed depth: 6–13mm (¼–½in)

Soil temperature: 10–35°C (50–95°F); the optimum is 29°C (85°F)

Days to germination: 2–5

Sow indoors: Not recommended

Sow outdoors: Early spring to midsummer

GROWING

pH range: 5.5–6.8

Soil temperature: 4–24°C (40–75°F); the optimum is 16°C (60°F)

Spacing in beds: 10cm (4in)

Watering: Moderate

Light: Best in full sun; tolerates light shade

Nutrient requirements: N=low; P=low; K=low

Rotation considerations: Avoid following cabbage family crops

Good companions: Onion family, pea

Bad companions: Potato

Seed longevity: 4 years

Seeds per gram: 500 (14,000 seeds per oz)

Suppliers

BEANS AND HERBS
The Herbary, 161 Chapel Street, Horningsham
Warminster, Wiltshire, BA12 7LU
Website: www.beansandherbs.co.uk
Specialist supplier of organic and heirloom bean
and herb seeds; also green manure seeds

CHILTERN SEEDS
Bortree Stile, Ulverston, Cumbria, LA12 7PB
Phone: 01229 581137
Fax: 01229 584549
Website: www.chilternseeds.co.uk
Organic, heirloom and oriental vegetable
seeds, and culinary herb seeds

DOBIES OF DEVON
Long Road, Paignton, Devon, TQ4 7SX
Phone (orders): 0870 1123625
Phone (customer services): 0870 112 3623
Fax: 0870 1123624
Website: www.dobies.co.uk
Seeds and garden supplies

FERNDALE LODGE
Ferndale Lodge, Woodview Road,
Paignton, Devon, TQ4 7NG
Phone: 0870 444 1342
Fax: 0870 444 0826
Website: www.ferndale-lodge.co.uk
Garden equipment, including propagators,
plant protection and hand tools

THE GREENHOUSE PEOPLE LTD
Blythe Park, Cresswell, Stoke-on-Trent,
Staffordshire, ST11 9RD
Phone: 0870 442 2328
Fax: 01782 388811
Website: www.thegreenhousepeople.co.uk
Greenhouses, cold frames, row tunnels and
propagators

MARSHALLS SEEDS
Wisbech, Cambridgeshire, PE13 2RF
Website: www.marshalls-seeds.co.uk
Large range of vegetable seeds from this old firm

MR FOTHERGILL'S SEEDS
Gazeley Road, Kentford,
Newmarket, Suffolk, CB8 7QB
Phone: 01638 751161
Fax: 01638 554084
Website: www.mr-fothergills.co.uk
Vegetable and herb seeds

NICKY'S NURSERY
33, Fairfield Road, Broadstairs, Kent, CT10 2JU
Phone and Fax: 01843 600972
Website: www.nickys-nursery.co.uk/seed
Rare and unusual vegetable seeds, including an
exceptional tomato list; garden sundries

THE REAL SEED CATALOGUE
Brithdir Mawr Farm, Newport, Fishguard,
Pembrokeshire, SA42 0QJ
Phone: 01239 821107
Website: www.realseeds.co.uk
Many heirloom and unusual vegetable seeds;
no hybrids

SEEDS OF ITALY
C3, Phoenix Industrial Estate, Rosslyn
Crescent, Harrow, Middlesex, HA1 2SP
Tel: 0208 427 5020
Fax: 0208 427 5051
Website: www.seedsofitaly.com
Seeds of continental salad crops, and more

SUTTONS
Woodview Rd, Paignton, Devon, TQ4 7NG
Phone (customer services): 0870 2202899
Phone (orders): 0870 220 0606
Fax: 0870 2202265
Website: www.suttons.seeds.co.uk
Seeds and garden equipment

TAMAR ORGANICS
Cartha Martha Farm, Rezare,
Launceston, Cornwall, PL15 9NX
Phone and Fax: 01579 371087
Website: www.tamarorganics.co.uk
Organic vegetable seeds and garden supplies

THOMPSON AND MORGAN
SEEDS (UK) LTD
Poplar Lane, Ipswich, Suffolk, IP8 3BU
Customer Care: 01473 688821
Switchboard: 01473 695200
Fax: 01473 680199
Website: www.seeds.thompson-morgan.com/uk
A large list of unusual seed varieties

TUCKER'S SEEDS
Brewery Meadow, Stonepark, Ashburton,
Newton Abbot, Devon, TQ13 7DG
Phone: 01364 652233
Fax: 01364 654211

Website: www.edwintucker.com
A huge range of seed potatoes varieties

TWO WESTS & ELLIOTT LTD
Unit 4, Carrwood Road, Sheepbridge Ind. Estate,
Chesterfield, Derbyshire, S41 9RH
Phone: 0870 444 8274
Fax: 01246 260115
Website: www.TwoWests.co.uk
Garden equipment, including cloches, row
covers, cold frames and propagators

Further Reading

BIGGS, Tony. *Growing Vegetables (The Royal Horticultural Encyclopedia of Practical Gardening)*. Mitchell Beazley, 1999.
A clearly illustrated, practical guide to all the technical aspects of vegetable gardening.

BIOSSET, Caroline. *Pumpkins and Squashes*. Mitchell Beazley, 1997.
Written by an enthusiast.

BLEASDALE, J.K.A., and others. *Know and Grow Vegetables*. Oxford University Press, 1991.
This book tells you about the scientific basis of vegetable growing: why it recommends certain plant spacings, or a particular watering regime. Can be eye-opening.

HICHMOTT, Simon. *Growing Unusual Vegetables*. Eco-Logic Books, 2004.
A good book for gardeners who want to push the boundaries.

HOPP, Henry. *What Every Gardener Should Know About Earthworms*. Country Wisdom Bulletin A-21, Storey Publishing, 1978.
This concise booklet provides just the information its title says it will.

LARKCOM, Joy. *Grow Your Own Vegetables*. Frances Lincoln, 2002.
This is a comprehensive and up-to-date guide, providing an enormous amount of detailed, practical information on growing a very wide range of vegetables.

LARKCOM, Joy. *The Organic Salad Guide*. Frances Lincoln, 2005.
An updated classic, this is a guide which covers all aspects of growing over 200 salad plants, including information about selecting for flavour.

MCMILLAN BROWSE, Philip. *Plant Propagation (The Royal Horticultural Encyclopedia of Practical Gardening)*. Mitchell Beazley, 1999.
An excellent guide to every kind of plant propagation (not only of vegetables), with clear illustrations of the various techniques.

OGDEN, Shepherd. *Straight-Ahead Organic*. Chelsea Green Publishing Company, 1999.
A clear introduction to organic gardening; especially good on pesticides and the GMO debate.

Index